PEARSON

REALITY CENTRAL

Real World Writing Journal

D0813559

PEARSON

Upper Saddle River, New Jersey • Boston, Massachusetts
Chandler, Arizona • Glenview, Illinois • Shoreview, Minnesota

ISBN-13: 978-0-13-367514-6

ISBN-10: 0-13-367514-9

8 9 10 V011 12 11

TABLE OF CONTENTS

About Your Book iv

Unit 1 1

Unit 2 35

Unit 3 69

Unit 4 103

Unit 5 137

Unit 6 155

Grammar, Usage, and Mechanics Handbook 189

Editing Checklist 227

Proofreaders' Marks 228

Personal Word Bank 229

ABOUT YOUR BOOK

The What and Why of This Book

This book is designed to help you develop strategies you can use while learning about writing, grammar, usage, and vocabulary. While you write and work with vocabulary, you will return to the articles in your Student Anthology. You will think more deeply about the Big Questions.

Write About It!

Each article in your Student Anthology has an opportunity for you to Write About It! A writing assignment helps you think about the Big Question in a new way.

Draft It
A writing frame helps you organize your writing.

Writing Prompt
A prompt explains the assignment.

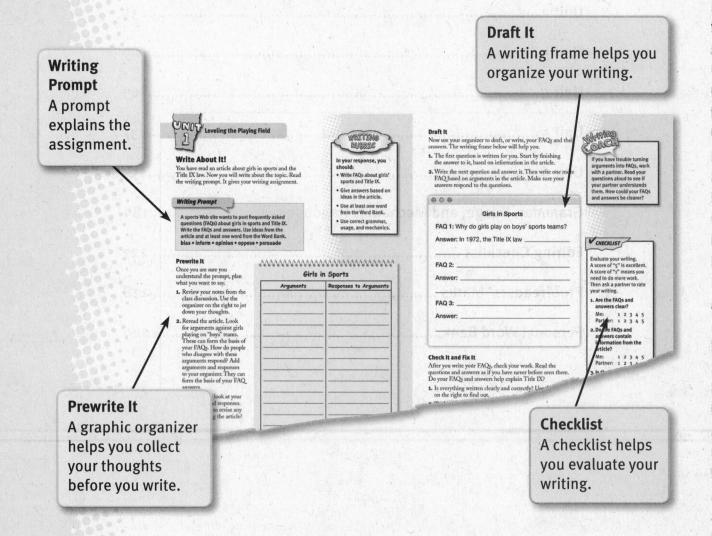

Prewrite It
A graphic organizer helps you collect your thoughts before you write.

Checklist
A checklist helps you evaluate your writing.

Vocabulary Workshop

Each article in your Student Anthology has a Vocabulary Workshop. In the workshop, you explore words from the Word Bank as you use them in different ways. Expanding your vocabulary will help you become a better reader and writer.

Your Choice
Record other words you want to remember.

Show You Know
Check your understanding about words by writing stories, crafting clues, or answering questions.

Define It
Graphic organizers help you expand your thinking about words.

Word Parts
Finding out about word parts will help you figure out words you may not know.

All In The Family
Explore variations of words that are all in the same family.

Partner Up
Use these suggestions for working with partners.

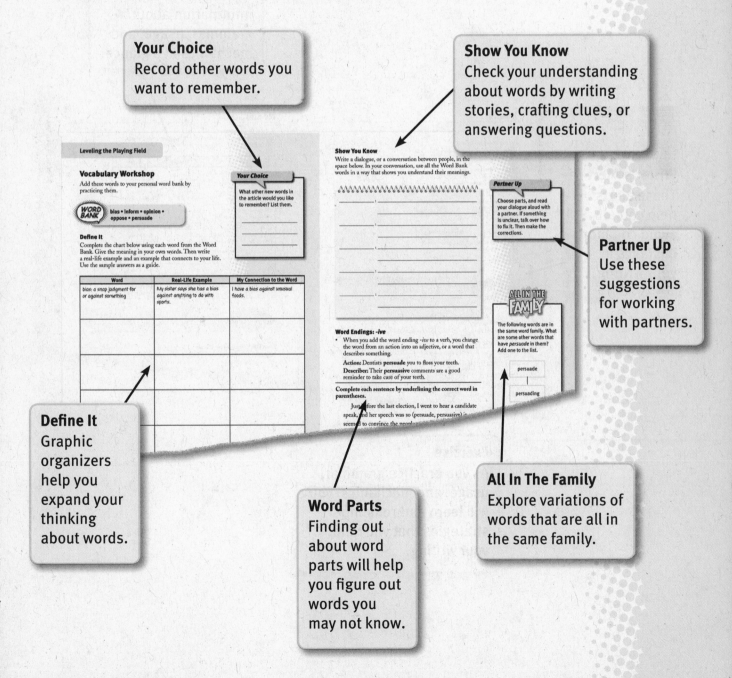

Grammar, Usage, and Mechanics Handbook

The Grammar, Usage, and Mechanics Handbook answers questions you may have during and after writing. It will help you correctly write and punctuate sentences. It will help you spell words that are commonly misspelled or confused.

Charts
Charts like this one help you find useful information about grammar, usage, and mechanics at a glance.

Writer's Alert
These alerts help you avoid common mistakes in your writing.

Exercise
As you practice grammar, usage, and mechanics, you will learn and remember strategies that will help your writing.

GRAMMAR HANDBOOK

Nouns

A noun names a person, a place, or a thing.

Person: Mona is a student.
Place: My school is Marson Middle School.
Thing: That article is about baseball.

Regular Plurals
A **singular noun** names one person, place, or thing.
A **plural noun** names more than one person, place, or thing.
To form the plural of most nouns, add -s to the end of the noun.

Singular	Plural
one teenager	two teenagers
this computer	these computers
that government	those governments
a site	many sites

 WRITER'S ALERT! A noncount noun, which names something you cannot count, does not have a plural form. Some common noncount nouns are *clothing, equipment, furniture, information, knowledge,* and *water.*

Exercise: Regular Plurals
Highlight and fix the five mistakes in noun plurals.
(1) Roger Jensen was the first of many storm chaser. (2) They like to take photograph of thunderstorms and twisters. (3) Some individuals also enjoy the thrill of chasing hurricane. (4) Several weather station provide information to storm chasers. (5) Most individuals who chase do not get paid. (6) Over the last ten year, the Internet has led to an increased interest in storm chasing.

GRAMMAR HANDBOOK

Nouns continued

Special Noun Plurals
To make some nouns plural, you need to do more than add an -s ending. Use the chart to figure out how to spell these plurals.

Singular Noun Ending	Singular	Plural
When a noun ends in *ch, s, sh, x,* or *z,* add *-es.*	a lunch one dress that dish this box each waltz	two lunches many dresses those dishes these boxes several waltzes
When a noun ends in a consonant + *y,* change the *y* to *i* and add *-es.*	a country one penny every city	many countries several pennies ten cities
When a noun ends in *f* or *fe,* change the *f* to *v* and add *-es.* Note exceptions to this rule.	this leaf one knife a chief one roof	these leaves two knives several chiefs many roofs
When a noun ends in a consonant + *o,* add *-es.* Note exceptions to this rule.	that hero a potato one piano an auto	those heroes a dozen potatoes many pianos several autos

WRITER'S ALERT! Do not use an apostrophe to form the plural of a noun. **Wrong:** many belief's **Right:** many beliefs

Exercise: Special Noun Plurals
Highlight the misspelled noun plural in each sentence. Then fix the spelling mistake. Use the chart or a dictionary for help.
(1) Hurricanes

 Is truth the same for everyone?

Leveling the Playing Field
Write About It! FAQs (Frequently Asked Questions) 2
Vocabulary Workshop 4

Separate Justice
Write About It! Judge's Decision 6
Vocabulary Workshop 8

This Land Is *Whose* Land?
Write About It! Paragraph 10
Vocabulary Workshop 12

Laws That Work for Kids Who Work
Write About It! Persuasive Speech 14
Vocabulary Workshop 16

Debating the Ratings
Write About It! Editorial 18
Vocabulary Workshop 20

The CSI Effect
Write About It! Advice Letter.. 22
Vocabulary Workshop 24

At First Sight
Write About It! Narrative 26
Vocabulary Workshop 28

American Dreaming
Write About It! Interview Report 30
Vocabulary Workshop 32

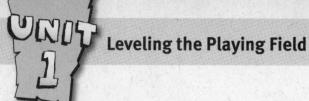

UNIT 1 Leveling the Playing Field

Write About It!

You have read an article about girls in sports and the Title IX law. Now you will write about the topic. Read the writing prompt. It gives your writing assignment.

Writing Prompt

A sports Web site wants to post frequently asked questions (FAQs) about girls in sports and Title IX. Write the FAQs and answers. Use ideas from the article and at least one word from the Word Bank.

bias • inform • opinion • oppose • persuade

Prewrite It

Once you are sure you understand the prompt, plan what you want to say.

1. Review your notes from the class discussion. Use the organizer on the right to jot down your thoughts.

2. Reread the article. Look for arguments against girls playing on "boys" teams. These can form the basis of your FAQs. How do people who disagree with these arguments respond? Add arguments and responses to your organizer. They can form the basis of your FAQ answers.

3. Take another look at your arguments and responses. Do you need to revise any after rereading the article?

WRITING RUBRIC

In your response, you should:

• Write FAQs about girls' sports and Title IX.

• Give answers based on ideas in the article.

• Use at least one word from the Word Bank.

• Use correct grammar, usage, and mechanics.

Girls in Sports

Arguments	Responses to Arguments

Draft It

Now use your organizer to draft, or write, your FAQs and their answers. The writing frame below will help you.

1. The first question is written for you. Start by finishing the answer to it, based on information in the article.

2. Write the next question and answer it. Then write one more FAQ based on arguments in the article. Make sure your answers respond to the questions.

If you have trouble turning arguments into FAQs, work with a partner. Read your questions aloud to see if your partner understands them. How could your FAQs and answers be clearer?

Girls in Sports

FAQ 1: Why do girls play on boys' sports teams?

Answer: In 1972, the Title IX law _____

_____

FAQ 2: _____

Answer: _____

_____

FAQ 3: _____

Answer: _____

_____

Check It and Fix It

After you write your FAQs, check your work. Read the questions and answers as if you have never before seen them. Do your FAQs and answers help explain Title IX?

1. Is everything written clearly and correctly? Use the checklist on the right to find out.

2. Trade your work with a classmate. Talk over ways you both might improve your FAQs and answers. Use new ideas from your discussion to revise your work.

3. For help with grammar, usage, and mechanics, go to the Handbook on pages 189–226.

✔ **CHECKLIST**

Evaluate your writing. A score of "5" is excellent. A score of "1" means you need to do more work. Then ask a partner to rate your writing.

1. Are the FAQs and answers clear?

Me: 1 2 3 4 5
Partner: 1 2 3 4 5

2. Do the FAQs and answers contain information from the article?

Me: 1 2 3 4 5
Partner: 1 2 3 4 5

3. Is there at least one word from the Word Bank?

Me: 1 2 3 4 5
Partner: 1 2 3 4 5

4. Are grammar, usage, and mechanics correct?

Me: 1 2 3 4 5
Partner: 1 2 3 4 5

Vocabulary Workshop

Add these words to your personal word bank by practicing them.

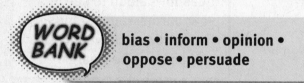 bias • inform • opinion • oppose • persuade

Your Choice

What other new words in the article would you like to remember? List them.

_____

_____

_____

Define It

Complete the chart below using each word from the Word Bank. Give the meaning in your own words. Then write a real-life example and an example that connects to your life. Use the sample answers as a guide.

Word	Real-Life Example	My Connection to the Word
bias: a snap judgment for or against something	My sister says she has a bias against anything to do with sports.	I have a bias against unusual foods.

Show You Know

Write a dialogue, or a conversation between people, in the space below. In your conversation, use all the Word Bank words in a way that shows you understand their meanings.

_____ : _____

_____

_____ : _____

_____

_____ : _____

_____

_____ : _____

_____

_____ : _____

_____

Partner Up

Choose parts, and read your dialogue aloud with a partner. If something is unclear, talk over how to fix it. Then make the corrections.

Word Endings: *-ive*

- When you add the word ending *-ive* to a verb, you change the word from an action into an adjective, or a word that describes something.

  Action: Dentists **persuade** you to floss your teeth.

  Describer: Their **persuasive** comments are a good reminder to take care of your teeth.

Complete each sentence by underlining the correct word in parentheses.

Just before the last election, I went to hear a candidate speak, and her speech was so (persuade, persuasive) it seemed to convince the people near me. Every point she made was meant to (persuade, persuasive) the audience that she would help pass laws to benefit us. I knew she was (persuade, persuasive).

The following words are in the same word family. What are some other words that have *persuade* in them? Add one to the list.

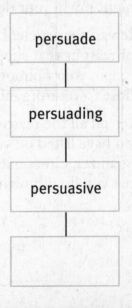

UNIT 1 Separate Justice

WRITING RUBRIC

Write About It!

You have read an article about how two different justice systems deal with young people accused of crimes. Now you will write about the topic. Read the writing prompt. It gives your writing assignment.

Writing Prompt

Imagine that for the third time, the same teenager has broken the law. He has already been tried twice in juvenile court. Should he go to an adult court this time? Write a judge's decision. Use ideas from the article and at least one word from the Word Bank.

contradict • doubtful • observation • represent • theory

In your response, you should:

- Write your decision in a paragraph.
- Use ideas from the article.
- Use at least one word from the Word Bank.
- Use correct grammar, usage, and mechanics.

Prewrite It

Once you are sure you understand the prompt, plan what you want to say.

1. Review your notes from the class discussion. Use the organizer on the right to jot down ideas about what you might say in your decision.

2. Reread the article. Look for reasons that support or explain your opinion. Add those to your organizer.

3. Reread all the reasons you have listed on your organizer. Cross out reasons that you do not plan to use.

Judge's Decision

My Decision

Your decision states which court you would choose.

My Reasons

Your reasons explain your decision.

Draft It

Now use your organizer to draft, or write, your decision. The writing frame below will help you.

1. Start by stating your decision. Underline which court you would send the teen to.

2. Read the second sentence below. Finish the thought by giving a good reason. Then add other reasons.

> ### Judge's Decision
>
> It is my final decision that the teen should be tried in
>
> (juvenile court, adult court). I have made this ruling because
>
> _____
>
> _____
>
> _____
>
> _____
>
> _____
>
> _____
>
> _____
>
> _____
>
> _____

Writing COACH

If you have trouble writing reasons for your decision, work with a partner. Tell your partner why you chose a particular court. Have him or her take notes, and use them to write.

Check It and Fix It

After you have written your decision, check your work. Imagine that you have never before thought about this issue. Are your reasons convincing?

1. Is everything written clearly and correctly? Use the checklist on the right to find out.

2. Exchange judge's decisions with a classmate. Discuss ways you both might improve your judge's decisions. Use the new ideas to revise your work.

3. For help with grammar, usage, and mechanics, go to the Handbook on pages 189–226.

✓ CHECKLIST

Evaluate your writing. A score of "5" is excellent. A score of "1" means you need to do more work. Then ask a partner to rate your writing.

1. **Is it clear to which court the teen will be sent?**

   Me: 1 2 3 4 5
   Partner: 1 2 3 4 5

2. **Do ideas from the article help explain the decision?**

   Me: 1 2 3 4 5
   Partner: 1 2 3 4 5

3. **Is there at least one word from the Word Bank?**

   Me: 1 2 3 4 5
   Partner: 1 2 3 4 5

4. **Are grammar, usage, and mechanics correct?**

   Me: 1 2 3 4 5
   Partner: 1 2 3 4 5

Vocabulary Workshop

Add these words to your personal word bank by practicing them.

WORD BANK contradict • doubtful • observation • represent • theory

Define It

For each set of boxes below, do as follows. Choose two words from the Word Bank and write them in the small boxes. (One word will appear twice.) In the Connection box, describe how the two words are connected. Use the example as a guide.

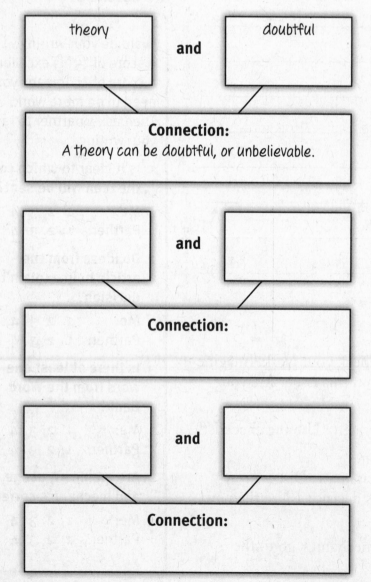

theory   and   doubtful

Connection:
A theory can be doubtful, or unbelievable.

and

Connection:

and

Connection:

Word COACH

Look for connections between new words. Connections can help you use and remember new vocabulary.

Show You Know

Answer the questions below to show you know the meaning of each Word Bank word.

1. If you **contradict** someone during an argument, do you agree with the person? Explain why or why not.

   _____

2. Why might a student who has not studied look **doubtful** during a test?

   _____

3. The doctor did not know the boy's problem, so she put him under **observation**. What did she do?

   _____

4. A symbol might **represent** something else. Why?

   _____

5. A **theory** is not always true. Why not?

   _____

Root Words: *dict*

- Root words can help you understand unfamiliar words. The root *dict-* comes from a Latin word meaning "to speak or say."

For each sentence, underline the root in the boldface word. Use the root and other clues to write what each word means.

1. The speaker planned to **dictate** what the rules would be.

Meaning: _____

_____

2. No one can **predict** how the weather might change.

Meaning: _____

_____

Separate Justice   **9**

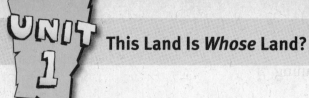

UNIT 1 — This Land Is *Whose* Land?

Write About It!

You have read an article about eminent domain, which is the taking of private property for public use. Now you will write about the topic. Read the writing prompt. It gives your writing assignment.

WRITING RUBRIC

In your response, you should:

- Give your opinion about the plan to tear down a senior center.
- Give reasons based on the article.
- Use at least one word from the Word Bank.
- Use correct grammar, usage, and mechanics.

Writing Prompt

Imagine that your school wants to build an addition. To make room for it, the town plans to tear down a senior center next door. Is that right? In a paragraph, tell what you think and why. Use ideas from the article and at least one word from the Word Bank.

arrange • evidence • fantasy • investigate • prove

Prewrite It

Once you are sure you understand the prompt, plan what you want to say.

1. Review your notes from the class discussion. Use the organizer on the right to jot down your thoughts.

2. Reread the article. Look for additional reasons that support or explain your opinion. Add those to your organizer.

3. Take another look at your opinion. Do you need to change it after rereading the article? If so, make the changes. Read the reasons you have listed. Which are the best? Cross out reasons that are not as good.

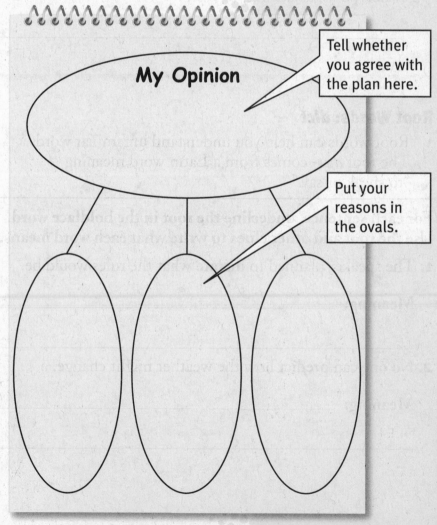

My Opinion

Tell whether you agree with the plan here.

Put your reasons in the ovals.

Draft It

Now use your organizer to draft, or write, a paragraph. The writing frame below will help you.

1. Start by stating your opinion about the plan. Read the first sentence, below. Underline your opinion.

2. Write your reasons. Read the second sentence below. Finish the thought by giving the best reason for your opinion. Then add other reasons.

Taking a Stand

I (agree, do not agree) that destroying our town's senior-citizen center is necessary in order to build an addition to our school. I feel this way because _____

_____

_____

_____

_____

_____

_____

_____

Check It and Fix It

After you have written your paragraph, check your work. Try to read it with a "fresh eye," as if you have not seen it before.

1. Is everything written clearly and correctly? Use the checklist on the right to find out.

2. Trade paragraphs with a partner. Talk over ways you both might improve your paragraphs. Use your partner's ideas to revise your work.

3. For help with grammar, usage, and mechanics, go to the Handbook on pages 189–226.

If you have trouble explaining your opinion, work with a partner. Tell your partner what you think. Ask the person to help you word your ideas so that you can write them.

✔ CHECKLIST

Evaluate your writing. A score of "5" is excellent. A score of "1" means you need to do more work. Then ask a partner to rate your writing.

1. **Does the paragraph clearly state an opinion about the building plan?**

   Me: 1 2 3 4 5
   Partner: 1 2 3 4 5

2. **Is the opinion supported by good reasons from the article?**

   Me: 1 2 3 4 5
   Partner: 1 2 3 4 5

3. **Is there at least one word from the Word Bank?**

   Me: 1 2 3 4 5
   Partner: 1 2 3 4 5

4. **Are grammar, usage, and mechanics correct?**

   Me: 1 2 3 4 5
   Partner: 1 2 3 4 5

This Land Is *Whose* Land?   **11**

Vocabulary Workshop

Add these words to your personal word bank by practicing them.

arrange • evidence • fantasy • investigate • prove

Your Choice

What other new words in the article would you like to remember? List them.

_____

_____

_____

Define It

In your own words, write what each word in the Word Bank means. Then think of a word that has the same or a very similar meaning. Write that word as shown in the example below.

What It Means	fantasy
something you pretend or imagine	**A Word It Reminds Me Of** daydream
What It Means	
	A Word It Reminds Me Of _____
What It Means	
	A Word It Reminds Me Of _____
What It Means	
	A Word It Reminds Me Of _____
What It Means	
	A Word It Reminds Me Of _____

Show You Know

In the space below, write a short, short story (just a paragraph!) using the Word Bank words. Be sure your sentences show that you understand the meanings of the words.

Once upon a time, _____

_____

_____

_____

_____

_____

Word Endings: *-ment*

- When you add the word ending *-ment* to a verb, you change the word from an action into a thing, or noun.

  Verb: I had to **arrange** all the papers in my folder so I could see when my homework was due.

  Noun: The new **arrangement** helped me stay organized.

Complete each sentence by underlining the correct word in parentheses.

Jessie watched her sister Anne (arrange, arrangement) the flowers in the vase. At first, she did not know how the (arrange, arrangement) might turn out. But Anne knew how to (arrange, arrangement) them beautifully. The final (arrange, arrangement) was colorful and pleasing.

The following words are in the same word family. What are some other words that have *arrange* in them? Add one to the list.

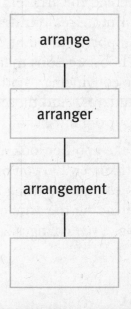

arrange

arranger

arrangement

This Land Is *Whose* Land?   **13**

Write About It!

You have read an article about work laws for young people. Now you will write about the topic. Read the writing prompt. It gives your writing assignment.

Writing Prompt

Imagine that your school is holding a debate and that you have been invited to take part in it. The debate question is as follows: Do teen workers need the protection of special laws? Write a short persuasive speech answering the question. Use ideas from the article and at least one word from the Word Bank.

doubtful • factual • illogical • objective • variation

WRITING RUBRIC

In your response, you should:

- Write a speech about special work laws.

- Include reasons explained in the article.

- Use at least one word from the Word Bank.

- Use correct grammar, usage, and mechanics.

Prewrite It

Once you are sure you understand the prompt, plan what you want to say.

1. Review your notes from the class discussion. Use the organizer on the right to jot down ideas.

2. Reread the article. Look for more reasons that support your point of view. Choose reasons that will be convincing to other students. Add those to your organizer.

3. Take another look at your organizer. Do you need to change anything after rereading the article? If so, make the changes.

Speech Plan

What I Think	Why Students Should Agree

Draft It

Now use your organizer to draft, or write, your speech. The writing frame below will help you.

1. Start by restating the debate question and giving your point of view. Read the first two sentences below. Underline the point of view that you agree with.

2. Then read sentence three. It introduces the "reasons" part of your speech. Add your reasons on the lines provided.

If you have trouble deciding what reasons to give, talk them over with classmates. They are the people you are trying to convince, so listen to what they have to say.

Debate Speech

Do teen workers need the protection of special laws? I say

(yes, no), and you should agree. Here is why. _____

_____

_____

_____

_____

_____

_____

_____

_____

_____

✔ CHECKLIST

Evaluate your writing.
A score of "5" is excellent.
A score of "1" means you need to do more work.
Then ask a partner to rate your writing.

1. **Does the speech give a point of view about teen work laws?**

   Me: 1 2 3 4 5
   Partner: 1 2 3 4 5

2. **Are there convincing reasons for the point of view?**

   Me: 1 2 3 4 5
   Partner: 1 2 3 4 5

3. **Is there at least one word from the Word Bank?**

   Me: 1 2 3 4 5
   Partner: 1 2 3 4 5

4. **Are grammar, usage, and mechanics correct?**

   Me: 1 2 3 4 5
   Partner: 1 2 3 4 5

Check It and Fix It

After you have written your speech, check your work. Try to read it as if you have never before seen it.

1. Is everything written clearly and correctly? Use the checklist on the right to see.

2. Deliver your speech to a classmate. Then listen to your partner's speech. Talk over ways you might improve your speeches. Use the new ideas to revise your speech.

3. For help with grammar, usage, and mechanics, go to the Handbook on pages 189–226.

Vocabulary Workshop

Add these words to your personal word bank by practicing them.

 **WORD BANK** doubtful • factual • illogical • objective • variation

Define It

Fill in the chart. In the center oval, write two or three subjects you could write about using the five Word Bank words. Use the examples as a model.

doubtful		
What It Means	**What It Means**	**What It Means**
not sure of something		
What It Means		**What It Means**

Subjects
Math: Might be doubtful about an answer.

Your Choice

What other new words in the article would you like to remember? List them.

_____

_____

_____

Word COACH

It is hard to remember new words if you do not know how to say them. If you cannot figure out how to pronounce a Word Bank word, ask your teacher or a classmate for help.

Show You Know

To show that you understand the Word Bank words, write a clue for each word. Exchange clues with a partner. See whether your partner can identify the correct word for each clue. Use the clue for the word *doubtful*, below, as a model.

- If you are not sure about something, you are this.

1. _____

2. _____

3. _____

4. _____

5. _____

Word Endings: -*ful*

- When you add the word ending -*ful* to a noun, you change the word from a thing into a describer, or adjective.

  Noun: I had no **doubt** I would play well at the concert.
  Adjective: Her **doubtful** look showed she did not practice before the concert.

Complete each sentence by underlining the correct word in parentheses.

When our soccer team lost, the players were filled with (doubt, doubtful). Our goalie was (doubt, doubtful) that he could prevent the other team from scoring. Our coach gave us a great pep talk, however, and soon we overcame our (doubt, doubtful).

The following words are in the same word family. What are some other words that have *doubt* in them? Add one to the list.

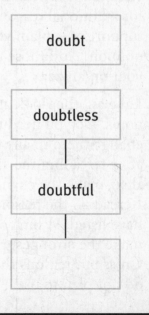

doubt

doubtless

doubtful

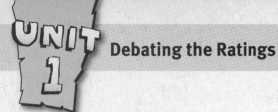

UNIT 1 Debating the Ratings

Write About It!

You have read an article about ratings for movies, video games, TV shows, and music. Now you will write about the topic. Read the writing prompt. It gives your writing assignment.

Writing Prompt

Imagine that you are a reporter for your school newspaper. Write an editorial stating your opinion about ratings for movies and other forms of entertainment. Use ideas from the article and at least one word from the Word Bank.

control • illogical • observation • opinion • theory

Prewrite It

Once you are sure you understand the prompt, plan what you want to say.

1. Review your notes from the class discussion. Use the organizer on the right to jot down your thoughts.

2. Reread the article. Look for additional reasons that support or explain your opinion. Add those to your organizer.

3. Take another look at your notes. Do you need to change them in any way after rereading the article? If so, make the changes. Reread all the reasons you have listed. Which ones make the strongest points? Cross out reasons that you do not plan to use.

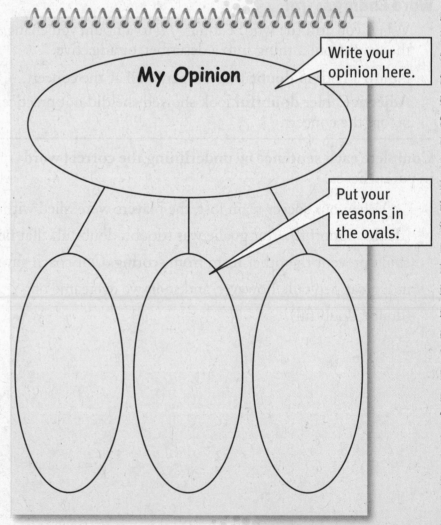

My Opinion

Write your opinion here.

Put your reasons in the ovals.

Draft It

Now use your organizer to draft, or write, an editorial. The writing frame below will help you.

1. On the blank line, write a headline, or title, for your article. In your headline, state whether you are for or against entertainment ratings.

2. Read the first sentence in the frame. It states the main idea of your editorial. Underline your opinion (either "good" or "bad").

3. Read the second sentence in the frame. Finish the thought with a strong reason. Write more reasons using ideas from the article.

THIS JUST IN

My headline: _____

Putting ratings on movies and other forms of

entertainment is a (good, bad) idea. I believe this because

_____

_____

_____

_____

_____

_____

_____

Check It and Fix It

After you have written your editorial, check your work. Try to read it as if you have never before seen it.

1. Is everything written clearly and correctly? Use the checklist on the right to see.

2. Trade editorials with a classmate. Talk over ways you might improve your editorials. Use the new ideas to revise your work.

3. For help with grammar, usage, and mechanics, go to the Handbook on pages 189–226.

✔ CHECKLIST

Evaluate your writing. A score of "5" is excellent. A score of "1" means you need to do more work. Then ask a partner to rate your writing.

1. **Does the editorial clearly state an opinion?**

   Me: 1 2 3 4 5
   Partner: 1 2 3 4 5

2. **Is the opinion supported with good reasons?**

   Me: 1 2 3 4 5
   Partner: 1 2 3 4 5

3. **Is there at least one word from the Word Bank?**

   Me: 1 2 3 4 5
   Partner: 1 2 3 4 5

4. **Are grammar, usage, and mechanics correct?**

   Me: 1 2 3 4 5
   Partner: 1 2 3 4 5

Vocabulary Workshop

Add these words to your personal word bank by practicing them.

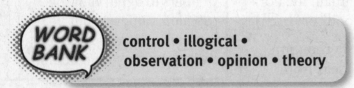

WORD BANK   control • illogical • observation • opinion • theory

Define It

Fill in the chart with the Word Bank words. In your own words, tell what each word means. Then circle the number that tells how well you understand each word. Circle "4" if you understand it completely. Circle "1" if you are not sure you understand the word at all. Use the example as a model.

What It Means	control	
to control something is to guide it or run it		**How Well I Understand It** 1 2 3 ④
What It Means		
		How Well I Understand It 1 2 3 4
What It Means		
		How Well I Understand It 1 2 3 4
What It Means		
		How Well I Understand It 1 2 3 4
What It Means		
		How Well I Understand It 1 2 3 4

Show You Know

Write a comic strip in the space below. Use all the Word Bank words in a way that shows you understand their meanings.

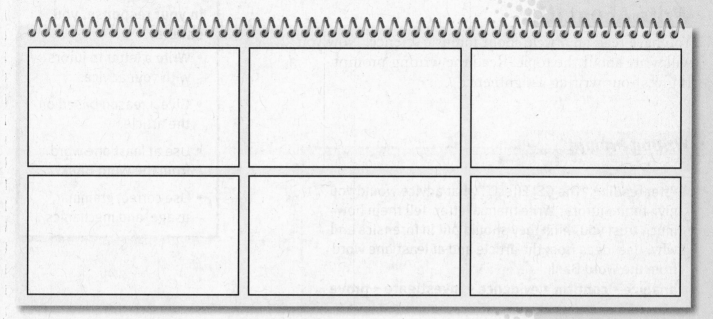

Word Beginnings: *il-*

- The prefix *il-* can mean "not," or "the opposite of." When you add *il-* to the beginning of a word, the word may mean the opposite of what it usually means.

   Example: I thought I gave a **logical** answer to the math problem, but my teacher said my answer was **illogical.**

Complete each sentence by underlining the correct word in parentheses.

The courtroom lawyer began to call witnesses to the stand, asking questions that followed (logical, illogical) patterns, so the jury could understand the issue. One witness told her story in a way that was (logical, illogical) just to confuse everyone. Though it is (legal, illegal) to have a bad memory, I wonder if it is (legal, illegal) for a witness to confuse people on purpose.

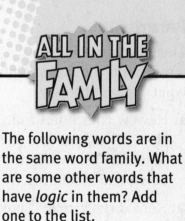

The following words are in the same word family. What are some other words that have *logic* in them? Add one to the list.

logic

logical

illogical

UNIT 1 — The CSI Effect

Write About It!

You have read an article about forensic science. Now you will write about the topic. Read the writing prompt. It gives your writing assignment.

Writing Prompt

After reading "The CSI Effect," what advice would you give future jurors? Write them a letter. Tell them how much trust you think they should put in forensics and why. Use ideas from the article and at least one word from the Word Bank.

analyze • confirm • evidence • investigate • prove

Prewrite It

Once you are sure you understand the prompt, plan what you want to say.

1. Review your notes from the class discussion. Use the organizer on the right to jot down your thoughts.

2. Reread the article. Look for additional reasons that support or explain your opinion. Add those to your organizer.

3. Take another look at your opinion. Do you need to change it in any way after rereading the article? If so, make the changes. Read through all the reasons you have listed. Which are the strongest? Cross out the reasons that are not as strong.

My Advice

My Opinion

Your opinion is your advice.

My Reasons

Your reasons explain your advice.

Draft It

Now use your organizer to draft, or write, a letter of advice. The writing frame below will help you.

1. Start by giving your opinion. You have three choices of opinion. Underline your choice.

2. Then give your reason. Read the second sentence below. Finish the thought by giving a reason for your opinion. Make sure you explain your reason with ideas from the article.

If you have trouble putting your ideas into words, work with a partner. Tell your partner what you want to say. Ask the person to write it down for you. Use the person's notes to write.

Dear Jurors:

I think you should put (all your trust, some trust, no trust)

in forensic science. I think this because _____

_____

_____

_____

_____

_____

_____

_____

_____

Check It and Fix It

After you have written your letter, check your work. Try to read it with a "fresh eye." Imagine you have never before read the letter.

1. Is everything written clearly and correctly? Use the checklist on the right to see.

2. Then trade letters with a classmate. Talk over ways you might improve your letters. Use the ideas to revise your work.

3. For help with grammar, usage, and mechanics, go to the Handbook on pages 189–226.

✔ CHECKLIST

Evaluate your writing. A score of "5" is excellent. A score of "1" means you need to do more work. Then ask a partner to rate your writing.

1. Does the letter give jurors clear advice?

Me: 1 2 3 4 5
Partner: 1 2 3 4 5

2. Do ideas from the article explain the advice?

Me: 1 2 3 4 5
Partner: 1 2 3 4 5

3. Is there at least one word from the Word Bank?

Me: 1 2 3 4 5
Partner: 1 2 3 4 5

4. Are grammar, usage, and mechanics correct?

Me: 1 2 3 4 5
Partner: 1 2 3 4 5

Vocabulary Workshop

Add these words to your personal word bank by practicing them.

WORD BANK   analyze • confirm • evidence • investigate • prove

Define It

Complete the chart below using the Word Bank words. First, tell what the word means. Then tell what the word does not mean. Use the example as a guide.

Word	What It Is	What It Is Not
analyze	separate a thing into parts, look at them carefully, and see how they fit together	look at a thing really fast without thinking about it

Your Choice

What other new words in the article would you like to remember? List them.

_____

_____

_____

Word COACH

The best way to remember new words is to use them. Use new words in and out of class. Use them when you think, talk, and write.

Show You Know

To show that you understand the Word Bank words, write three sentences. In each sentence, use and highlight two of the words. (You will use one word twice.) Use the example as a model.

- Detectives investigate crimes and look for evidence.

1. _____

   _____

2. _____

   _____

3. _____

   _____

Partner Up

Trade sentences with a partner. Check each other's sentences. If something needs fixing, talk over how to fix it. Then make corrections.

Word Endings: *-ion, -s*

- When you add the word ending *-ion* to a verb, you change the word from an action into a thing (a noun).

  Verb: Please **investigate** why the students were tardy.

  Noun: The **investigation** showed that the buses were late.

- When you add an *-s* ending to a verb, you make the verb match the singular subjects *he*, *she*, and *it*.

  Plural Subject: The teachers **investigate** why students are tardy.

  Singular Subject: The principal also **investigates** why students are tardy.

Complete each sentence by underlining the correct word in parentheses.

I watched a TV show about private detectives. These detectives (investigate, investigates, investigation) crimes for people and businesses rather than for the police. On the show, there is a private detective who (investigate, investigates, investigation) shoplifting. She does an (investigate, investigates, investigation) into ways to stop shoppers from stealing.

ALL IN THE FAMILY

The following words are in the same word family. What are some other words that have *investigate* in them? Add one to the list.

investigate

investigates

investigation

UNIT 1 At First Sight

WRITING RUBRIC

Write About It!

You have read an article about first impressions. Now you will write about the topic. Read the writing prompt. It gives your writing assignment.

Writing Prompt

Recall a time when you felt one way about someone you met, then later changed your opinion of the person. Write a short narrative telling how you felt and why your feelings changed. Use details from the article and at least one word from the Word Bank.

bias • confirm • factual • objective • process

In your response, you should:

- Write about a changed impression.
- Use details from the article.
- Use at least one word from the Word Bank.
- Use correct grammar, usage, and mechanics.

Prewrite It

Once you are sure you understand the prompt, plan what you want to say.

1. Review your notes from the class discussion. Use the organizer on the right to jot down ideas and details.

2. Reread the article. Look for additional details that might help explain your experiences. Add those to your organizer.

3. Take another look at your notes. Reread the ideas you have listed. Do you need to change them in any way after rereading the article? If so, make the changes.

First Meeting	Later Meeting or Meetings
First Impression	**Later Impression**

Draft It

Now use your organizer to draft, or write, your narrative. The writing frame below will help you.

1. Start by writing a title for your narrative.

2. To get started writing, read and fill in the first sentence.

3. Then "fast-forward" to a later meeting and describe your new impression. Include a reason why your impression changed. Use ideas from the article in your explanation.

To make your narrative come alive, use specific details. Include real-life dialogue, or write descriptions that appeal to the five senses. Describe sounds, sights, feelings, and so on.

My Title: _____

The first time I met _____ was

_____

_____.

My first impression was _____.

_____

_____

_____.

Later, my impression changed _____

_____

_____

_____.

Check It and Fix It

After you have written your narrative, check your work. Try to read it as if you have never before met the person. See if you have "painted" a clear picture of the person.

1. Is everything written clearly and correctly? Use the checklist on the right to see.

2. Trade narratives with a classmate. Talk over ways you both might improve your narratives. Use new ideas from your discussion to revise your narratives.

3. For help with grammar, usage, and mechanics, go to the Handbook on pages 189–226.

✔ **CHECKLIST**

Evaluate your writing. A score of "5" is excellent. A score of "1" means you need to do more work. Then ask a partner to rate your writing.

1. **Is the narrative about a changed impression?**

   Me: 1 2 3 4 5
   Partner: 1 2 3 4 5

2. **Are there ideas from the article?**

   Me: 1 2 3 4 5
   Partner: 1 2 3 4 5

3. **Is there at least one word from the Word Bank?**

   Me: 1 2 3 4 5
   Partner: 1 2 3 4 5

4. **Are grammar, usage, and mechanics correct?**

   Me: 1 2 3 4 5
   Partner: 1 2 3 4 5

Vocabulary Workshop

Add these words to your personal word bank by practicing them.

bias • confirm • factual • objective • process

Your Choice

What other new words in the article would you like to remember? List them.

_____

_____

_____

Define It

Complete the chart below using each word from the Word Bank. Give the meaning in your own words. Then write a real-life example and an example that connects to your life.

Word	Real-Life Example	My Connection to the Word

Show You Know

Answer the questions below to show you know the meaning of each Word Bank word.

Partner Up

Take turns with a partner, reading the questions and answering them. Do the answers show an understanding of the words? If not, help your partner rewrite them.

1. Would someone more likely have a **bias** against friends or enemies? Explain why. _____

   _____

2. How might you **confirm** when an assignment is due? _____

   _____

3. Who would be more likely to write something **factual**: a reporter or a poet? Explain why. _____

   _____

4. Why is it important for a teacher to be **objective**? _____

   _____

5. Name something you have to follow a **process** to do. _____

   _____

Action or Thing?

- Some words can show an action and can also refer to a thing. For example, the *process* can be an action you do or a thing that gets done.

  Action: The clerk had to **process** all the forms.

  Thing: Checking them was a difficult **process**.

The words *love* and *work* can also be verbs and nouns. Find another word in the article that can be an action and a thing. Write two sentences to show both meanings.

Action: _____

_____

Thing: _____

_____

Write About It!

You have read an article about the American Dream. Now you will write about the topic. Read the writing prompt. It gives your writing assignment.

Writing Prompt

Interview at least two classmates about their American Dreams. Use ideas from the article to help guide your questions. Then write a report about what your classmates said. Use ideas from the article and at least one word from the Word Bank.

contradict • equal • essential • fantasy • persuade

In your response, you should:

- Report classmates' ideas about their American Dreams.
- Use ideas from the article.
- Use at least one word from the Word Bank.
- Use correct grammar, usage, and mechanics.

Prewrite It

Once you are sure you understand the prompt, plan what you want to say.

1. Review notes from your class discussion. Use the organizer to jot down interview questions you want to ask.

2. Reread the article. Look for more ideas that might help you form your questions.

3. Look at your organizer again. Do you need to change your notes in any way after rereading the article? If so, make the changes. Are there additional topics you can use to question your classmates? If so, add them.

Interview Questions

Draft It

Now use your organizer to draft, or write, a report. The writing frame below will help you.

1. Start by asking each question on your list. Use a separate sheet of paper to take notes on classmates' answers.

2. Summarize your classmates' answers by completing the first sentence. Include similarities and differences in their answers.

3. Then give details. Refer to the article to see how the dreams might compare to those of other teens.

One Size Fits All Dreams?

After interviewing two classmates, I have found that the American Dream is

_____

_____

_____

_____

_____

_____

_____

_____

✔ **CHECKLIST**

Evaluate your writing. A score of "5" is excellent. A score of "1" means you need to do more work. Then ask a partner to rate your writing.

1. **Does the report clearly sum up what classmates said?**

   Me: 1 2 3 4 5
   Partner: 1 2 3 4 5

2. **Are ideas from the article used in the report?**

   Me: 1 2 3 4 5
   Partner: 1 2 3 4 5

3. **Is there at least one word from the Word Bank?**

   Me: 1 2 3 4 5
   Partner: 1 2 3 4 5

4. **Are grammar, usage, and mechanics correct?**

   Me: 1 2 3 4 5
   Partner: 1 2 3 4 5

Check It and Fix It

After you have written your report, check your work. Try to read it as if you were not the author.

1. Is everything written clearly and correctly? Use the checklist on the right to see.

2. Trade reports with a classmate. Talk over ways you both might improve your reports. Use new ideas from your discussion to improve your work.

3. For help with grammar, usage, and mechanics, go to the Handbook on pages 189–226.

Vocabulary Workshop

Add these words to your personal word bank by practicing them.

WORD BANK   contradict • equal • essential • fantasy • persuade

Define It

For each set of boxes below, do as follows. Choose two words from the Word Bank and write them in the small boxes. (One word will appear twice.) In the Connection box, describe how the two words are connected.

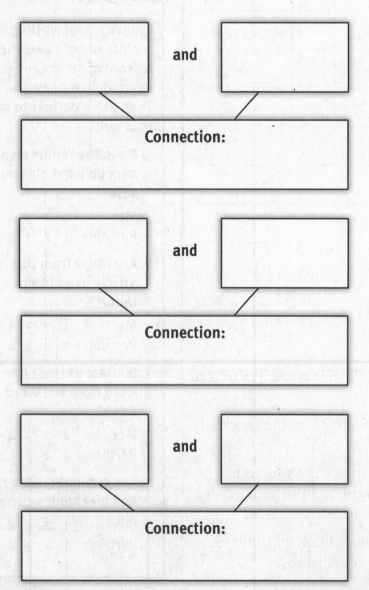

Show You Know

To show that you understand the Word Bank words, write a clue for each word. Exchange clues with a partner. See whether your partner can identify the correct word for each clue.

1. _____

2. _____

3. _____

4. _____

5. _____

Word Beginnings: *un-*

- When you add a prefix to a word, you change the word's meaning. The prefix *un-* is a reversal maker. Like the prefix *il-*, it means "not" or "the opposite of." Add *un-* to the following words and tell how the meanings change.

equal   unequal _____

               not the same, not fair _____

essential _____

      _____

limited _____

      _____

Complete each sentence by underlining the correct word in parentheses.

      Even though your talents may be (equal, unequal), everyone who wants to work on the school play will be given an (equal, unequal) chance. It is (essential, unessential) that you can act or sing, but it is (essential, unessential) that you come to rehearsals. Participation is (limited, unlimited) only by your desire to work hard.

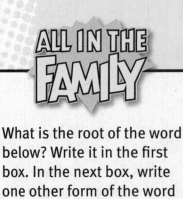

What is the root of the word below? Write it in the first box. In the next box, write one other form of the word that appears in the article.

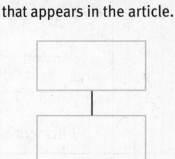

equality

Writing Reflection

 Is truth the same for everyone?

Look through your writing from this unit and choose the best piece. Reflect on this piece of writing by completing each sentence below.

My best piece of writing from this unit is _____

_____

I chose this piece because _____

_____

_____

While I was writing, one goal I had was _____

_____

I accomplished this goal by _____

_____

_____

This writing helped me think more about the Big Question because

_____

_____

One thing I learned while writing that can help me in the future is

_____

_____

Can all conflicts be resolved?

Games People Play
Write About It! Memo 36
Vocabulary Workshop 38

Cyber Friends
Write About It! Web Site Welcome Note 40
Vocabulary Workshop 42

Text Talk
Write About It! Guide to Text Messaging 44
Vocabulary Workshop 46

The Insanity Defense
Write About It! Letter 48
Vocabulary Workshop 50

Privacy vs. Safety
Write About It! Proposal 52
Vocabulary Workshop 54

The IQ Question
Write About It! Flyer 56
Vocabulary Workshop 58

The Curfew Question
Write About It! Speech 60
Vocabulary Workshop 62

Learning Character
Write About It! Invitation 64
Vocabulary Workshop 66

UNIT 2

Games People Play

WRITING RUBRIC

Write About It!

You have read an article about video games. Now you will write about the topic. Read the writing prompt. It gives your writing assignment.

Writing Prompt

After reading "Games People Play," what would you tell a video game designer? Write a memo to a designer about what you would like to see in a video game. Give the designer three guidelines the game should meet. Use ideas from the article and at least one word from the Word Bank.

compromise • detail • injury • interact • violence

In your response, you should:

- Write a memo to a video game designer.
- Use ideas from the article.
- Use at least one word from the Word Bank.
- Use correct grammar, usage, and mechanics.

Prewrite It

Once you are sure you understand the prompt, plan what you want to say.

1. Review your notes from the class discussion. Remind yourself of points that were made.

2. Reread the article. Look for features that you want the designer to include in the video game. Make notes on the organizer at the right.

3. Take another look at all the points you have listed. Do you think these are the most important points for the memo? If not, change them.

Video Game Memo

Guidelines	Reasons

Draft It

Now use your organizer to draft, or write, a memo to a video game designer. The writing frame below will help you.

1. In each paragraph, start by stating a guideline. You have two choices. Underline your choice.

2. Read the sentence starter in each paragraph. Finish the thought by giving reasons for your choices. Use ideas from the article.

To: Designer   Date:

From: Subject: New Game

Please make a video game about (sports, car racing). My reason is _____

_____.

Please make an (easy, hard) game. My reason is _____

_____.

Finally, please make a game played by (one person, a team). My reason is _____

_____.

✔ **CHECKLIST**

Evaluate your writing. A score of "5" is excellent. A score of "1" means you need to do more work. Then ask a partner to rate your writing.

1. **Does the memo state suggestions clearly?**

   Me: 1 2 3 4 5
   Partner: 1 2 3 4 5

2. **Are there ideas from the article that support each guideline?**

   Me: 1 2 3 4 5
   Partner: 1 2 3 4 5

3. **Is there at least one word from the Word Bank?**

   Me: 1 2 3 4 5
   Partner: 1 2 3 4 5

4. **Are grammar, usage, and mechanics correct?**

   Me: 1 2 3 4 5
   Partner: 1 2 3 4 5

Check It and Fix It

After you have written your memo, check your work. Imagine that you are seeing the memo for the first time.

1. Is your memo written clearly and correctly? Use the checklist on the right to see.

2. Trade memos with a classmate. Discuss how to improve your memos. Then revise your work.

3. For help with grammar, usage, and mechanics, go to the Handbook on pages 189–226.

Vocabulary Workshop

Add these words to your personal word bank by practicing them.

 **WORD BANK** compromise • detail • injury • interact • violence

Define It

Fill in the chart with the Word Bank words. In your own words, tell what each word means. Then circle the number that tells how well you understand each word. Circle "4" if you understand it completely. Circle "1" if you are not sure you understand the word at all. Use the example as a model.

What It Means	compromise
To compromise is to settle an argument by having both sides agree to something.	**How Well I Understand It** 1 2 3 ④
What It Means	
	How Well I Understand It 1 2 3 4
What It Means	
	How Well I Understand It 1 2 3 4
What It Means	
	How Well I Understand It 1 2 3 4
What It Means	
	How Well I Understand It 1 2 3 4

Your Choice

What other new words in the article would you like to remember? List them.

_____

_____

Word COACH

To remember new words, practice using them. Use a new word at least three times on the day you first study it. Try to use the word when you are talking and writing.

Show You Know

To show that you understand the Word Bank words, write a clue for each word. Exchange clues with a partner. See whether your partner can identify the correct word for each clue. Use the clue for the word *compromise*, below, as a model.

- When two people disagree, this can help make both of them happy.

1. _____

2. _____

3. _____

4. _____

5. _____

Word Beginnings: *inter-*

- A prefix, which is added to the beginning of a word, can be a clue to the meaning of the word. The prefix *inter-* means "between" or "among."

  You know the meaning of the Word Bank word *interact*. Can you see how the prefix works with the rest of the word to create that meaning?

Now answer the questions that contain words with the prefix *inter-*. Use the meaning of the prefix to understand the meanings of the words. Explain each answer.

1. Does something **international** happen among many countries or inside just one?

_____

2. Would you **interweave** a ribbon between the strands of your hair or around your head?

_____

3. Would **interconnected** streets run side by side, or would they cross each other?

_____

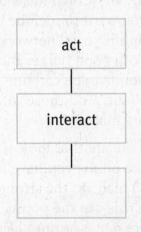

The following words are in the same word family. What are some other words that have *act* in them? Add one to the list.

act

interact

_____

Write About It!

You have read an article about pen pals on the Internet. Now you will write about the topic. Read the writing prompt. It gives your writing assignment.

Writing Prompt

After reading "Cyber Friends," what would you say to kids on a new social network Web site? Write a "Welcome to Our Site" note for a new Web site you are designing. You want to encourage kids to use your site, but you also want them to be safe. Use ideas from the article and at least one word from the Word Bank.

consider • insecurity • mislead • reveal • viewpoint

In your response, you should:

- Write a "Welcome to Our Site" note.

- Use information from the article.

- Use at least one word from the Word Bank.

- Use correct grammar, usage, and mechanics.

Prewrite It

Once you are sure you understand the prompt, plan what you want to say.

1. Review your notes from the class discussion. Use the organizer on the right to jot down your thoughts.

2. Reread the article. Look for additional ideas that you want to include about online social networks—both good points and points to be careful about. Add those to your organizer.

3. Take another look at all the points you have listed. Which are the strongest? Cross out the points that are not as strong. Decide what is most important to put in your welcome note.

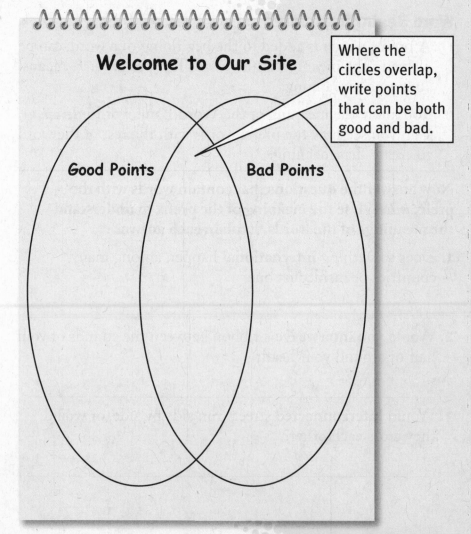

Welcome to Our Site

Good Points

Bad Points

Where the circles overlap, write points that can be both good and bad.

Draft It

Now use your organizer to draft, or write, a welcome note to a social network site. The writing frame below will help you.

1. Begin by writing the name of your site or the words *Our Site*.

2. Read each sentence starter. Then finish the sentence with a point from your organizer. Be sure to use information from the article.

○ ○ ○

Welcome to _____

Get to know people who _____

_____

_____.

You will enjoy special features such as _____

_____

_____.

Be careful, however, about _____

_____

_____.

Check It and Fix It

After you have written your note, check your work. Try to read it with a "fresh eye." Imagine that you have never before read the note.

1. Is your note clear? Have you written it correctly? The checklist on the right will help you see.

2. Trade notes with a classmate. Read each other's notes, and talk about how to improve them. Then revise your work.

3. For help with grammar, usage, and mechanics, go to the Handbook on pages 189–226.

Ask your partner to imagine that he or she is at your new Web site for the first time. Then ask if the welcome note is helpful. A response from a reader can help you decide whether your writing is effective.

✔ **CHECKLIST**

Evaluate your writing. A score of "5" is excellent. A score of "1" means you need to do more work. Then ask a partner to rate your writing.

1. **Does the note help the reader understand online social networks?**

   Me: 1 2 3 4 5
   Partner: 1 2 3 4 5

2. **Are ideas from the article used to make points?**

   Me: 1 2 3 4 5
   Partner: 1 2 3 4 5

3. **Is there at least one word from the Word Bank?**

   Me: 1 2 3 4 5
   Partner: 1 2 3 4 5

4. **Are grammar, usage, and mechanics correct?**

   Me: 1 2 3 4 5
   Partner: 1 2 3 4 5

Vocabulary Workshop

Add these words to your personal word bank by practicing them.

 **WORD BANK** consider • insecurity • mislead • reveal • viewpoint

Your Choice

What other new words in the article would you like to remember? List them.

_____

_____

_____

Define It

Fill in the chart. In the center oval, write two or three subjects you could write about using the Word Bank words. Use the examples as a model.

consider		
What It Means	**What It Means**	**What It Means**
think carefully about something		
What It Means		**What It Means**

Subjects
English: might consider
what a story means

Show You Know

Answer the questions below to show you know the meaning of each Word Bank word. Explain each answer.

1. Could you **consider** something in a split second? _____

_____

2. Would **insecurity** help you run for a school office? _____

_____

3. Would a commercial ever **mislead** you about a product? _____

_____

4. Do magicians **reveal** the secrets to their tricks? _____

_____

5. Does your **viewpoint** have anything to do with your opinions? _____

_____

Word Play

Using words with exact meanings can help you make your writing lively and specific. In the chart below, list some more words that mean the same or about the same as the Word Bank words. Think of words that have a precise meaning. Check a dictionary or thesaurus if you need to, and use the examples as models.

Word Bank Word	Words with Similar Meanings
consider	think, believe, judge
insecurity	anxiety, shyness, nervousness

UNIT 2 Text Talk

Write About It!

You have read an article about text messaging. Now you will write about the topic. Read the writing prompt. It gives your writing assignment.

Writing Prompt

After reading "Text Talk," what would you tell a parent about text messaging? Write a short guide to text messaging for parents. Explain what text messaging is and how it might help parents "talk" with their kids. Use ideas from the article and at least one word from the Word Bank.

irritate • respond • solution • substitute • victorious

Prewrite It

Once you are sure you understand the prompt, plan what you want to say.

1. Review your notes from the class discussion. Use the organizer on the right to start planning your text messaging guide.

2. Reread the article. Add notes about the important parts of the article.

3. Take another look at your notes. After rereading the article, is there anything important that you left out? If so, be sure to add it.

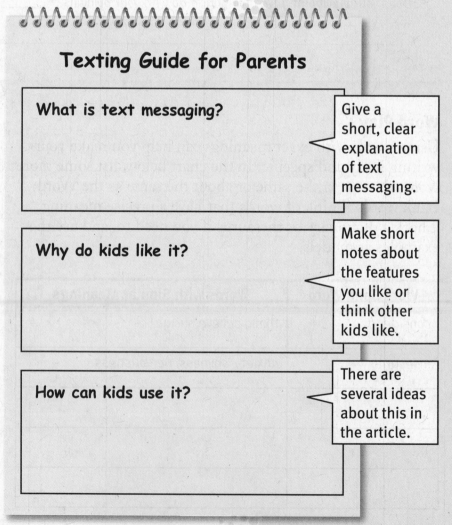

Texting Guide for Parents

What is text messaging?

> Give a short, clear explanation of text messaging.

Why do kids like it?

> Make short notes about the features you like or think other kids like.

How can kids use it?

> There are several ideas about this in the article.

Draft It

Now use your organizer to draft, or write, a short guide to text messaging for parents. The writing frame below will help you.

1. Use the sentence starters as an outline for your guide.

2. Finish the sentences with ideas you noted on your organizer. Be sure to include ideas from the article.

If you are not sure what the most important ideas are for your guide, talk them over with a partner. He or she may be able to remind you of something you have forgotten.

A Short Guide to Text Messaging

Text messaging is _____

_____

_____.

Kids like it because _____

_____

_____.

Texting can help you _____

_____

_____

Check It and Fix It

After you have finished your guide, check your work. Try to read it the way a parent would. Imagine that you have never before read a guide like this and the subject is new to you.

1. Is your guide clear? Have you written your ideas correctly? The checklist on the right will help you see.

2. Trade guides with a classmate. Talk about ways each of you might improve your guide. Use the ideas to revise your work.

3. For help with grammar, usage, and mechanics, go to the Handbook on pages 189–226.

✔ **CHECKLIST**

Evaluate your writing. A score of "5" is excellent. A score of "1" means you need to do more work. Then ask a partner to rate your writing.

1. **Does the guide communicate how text messaging works?**

   Me: 1 2 3 4 5
   Partner: 1 2 3 4 5

2. **Are points in the guide supported by ideas from the article?**

   Me: 1 2 3 4 5
   Partner: 1 2 3 4 5

3. **Is there at least one word from the Word Bank?**

   Me: 1 2 3 4 5
   Partner: 1 2 3 4 5

4. **Are grammar, usage, and mechanics correct?**

   Me: 1 2 3 4 5
   Partner: 1 2 3 4 5

Vocabulary Workshop

Add these words to your personal word bank by practicing them.

 **WORD BANK** irritate • respond • solution • substitute • victorious

Define It

Complete the chart below using the Word Bank words. First, tell what the word means. Then tell what the word does not mean. Use the example as a guide.

Word	What It Is	What It Is Not
irritate	to aggravate or annoy	to please someone or make someone happy

Your Choice

What other new words in the article would you like to remember? List them.

_____

_____

_____

Word COACH

To remember new words, write each on a note card. Write the definition on the back of the card and quiz yourself.

Show You Know

In the space below, write a short, short story (just a paragraph!) using the Word Bank words. Be sure your sentences show you understand the meanings of the words.

Once upon a time, _____

_____

_____

_____

_____

Partner Up

Trade stories with a partner. Check each other's sentences. If something needs fixing, talk over how to fix it. Then make corrections.

Word Sort

Fill in this chart with words from the Word Bank and the article. The chart is started for you.

Nouns	Verbs	Adjectives
solution	irritate	victorious

Now that you have sorted your words, pick two from different categories and use both in one sentence. For a challenge, use more than two of the words.

_____

_____

_____

_____

_____

Text Talk 47

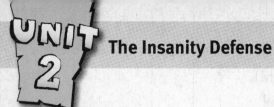

Write About It!

You have read an article about the insanity defense. Now you will write about the topic. Read the writing prompt. It gives your writing assignment.

WRITING RUBRIC

In your response, you should:

- Write a letter about the insanity plea.
- Use ideas from the article.
- Use at least one word from the Word Bank.
- Use correct grammar, usage, and mechanics.

Writing Prompt

After reading "The Insanity Defense," what do you think about the insanity plea? Write a letter to the attorney general of your state. Tell whether you think the insanity plea should be part of the state's legal system and why. Use ideas from the article and at least one word from the Word Bank.

compromise • detect • injury • negotiate • stalemate

Prewrite It

Once you are sure you understand the prompt, plan what you want to say.

1. Look at your notes from the class discussion. Write your opinion about the insanity plea in the organizer on the right.

2. Reread the article. Look for reasons that support your opinion. Add those to your organizer.

3. Take another look at your opinion and your reasons. Do you think your reasons are convincing? If not, think about how to improve them.

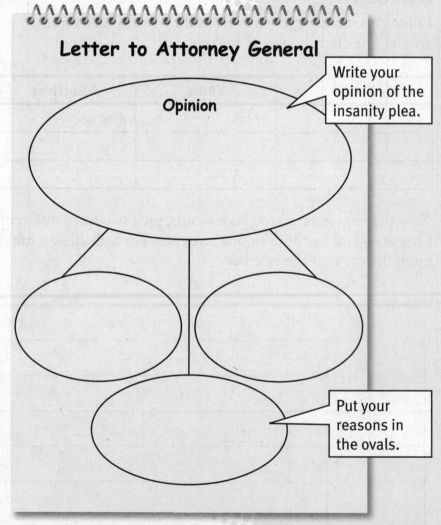

Letter to Attorney General

Opinion

Write your opinion of the insanity plea.

Put your reasons in the ovals.

Draft It

Now use your organizer to draft, or write, a letter to your state's attorney general. The writing frame below will help you.

1. Start by giving the attorney general your opinion. Underline the choice that you agree with.

2. Then support your opinion with your reasons. Make sure you explain your reasons with ideas and examples from the article.

Dear Attorney General:

　　Please work to make sure that the insanity plea (is, is not)

a part of our state law. My reasons for saying this are _____

_____

_____

_____

_____

_____

_____

_____

_____

_____ .

Talk to a classmate who disagrees with your opinion about the insanity plea. Explain your reasons and listen to his or hers. If you gave a reason that was not convincing, omit it from your letter.

Check It and Fix It

After you have written your letter, check your work. Imagine that you have never before read the letter, and see whether it makes sense to you. Would it help you decide about the insanity plea?

1. Did you write your letter clearly and correctly? The checklist on the right will help you see.

2. Exchange letters with a classmate. Talk about ways you both might improve your letters. Use the ideas to revise your work.

3. For help with grammar, usage, and mechanics, go to the Handbook on pages 189–226.

✔ CHECKLIST

Evaluate your writing. A score of "5" is excellent. A score of "1" means you need to do more work. Then ask a partner to rate your writing.

1. **Does the letter clearly state an opinion?**

   Me:　　1 2 3 4 5
   Partner: 1 2 3 4 5

2. **Are there ideas from the article to support the opinion?**

   Me:　　1 2 3 4 5
   Partner: 1 2 3 4 5

3. **Is there at least one word from the Word Bank?**

   Me:　　1 2 3 4 5
   Partner: 1 2 3 4 5

4. **Are grammar, usage, and mechanics correct?**

   Me:　　1 2 3 4 5
   Partner: 1 2 3 4 5

Vocabulary Workshop

Add these words to your personal word bank by practicing them.

 **WORD BANK** compromise • detect • injury • negotiate • stalemate

Your Choice

What other new words in the article would you like to remember? List them.

_____

_____

_____

Define It

Complete the chart below using each word from the Word Bank. Give the meaning in your own words. Then write a real-life example and an example that connects to your life. Use the sample answers on the chart as a guide.

Word	Real-Life Example	My Connection to the Word
compromise	The baseball-team owners and the players had to compromise so that there would not be a strike.	When I wanted a later bedtime, I had to compromise with my parents.

Show You Know

To show that you understand the Word Bank words, write a clue for each word. Exchange clues with a partner. See whether your partner can identify the correct word for each clue. Use the clue for the word *negotiate,* below, as a model.

- This is a way that people could decide on a price for something.

1. _____

2. _____

3. _____

4. _____

5. _____

Word Endings: *-ion, -s*

- When you add the word ending *-ion* to a verb, you change the word from an action into a thing, or noun.

  Verb: Sherlock Holmes could **detect** a lot from the smallest clue.

  Noun: He was a master of **detection.**

- When you add an *-s* to the end of a verb, you make the verb match a singular subject, such as *he, she,* or *it.*

  Plural Subject: Police officers **detect** the identity of a criminal.

  Singular Subject: This expert **detects** by studying fingerprints.

Complete each sentence by underlining the correct word in parentheses.

In one popular medical show, the doctor works like a private investigator, because she (detect, detects, detection) the causes of the patient's disease. Her (detect, detects, detection) does not stop with physical symptoms. She and her interns (detect, detects, detection) slight traces of poisons in the patient's backyard or in the food he or she has eaten.

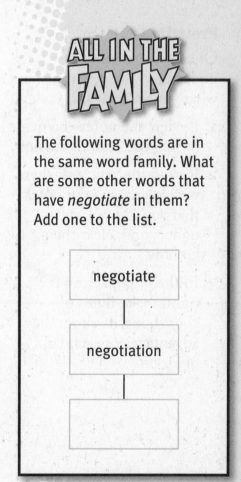

ALL IN THE FAMILY

The following words are in the same word family. What are some other words that have *negotiate* in them? Add one to the list.

| negotiate |
| negotiation |
| |

Write About It!

You have read an article about privacy and school lockers. Now you will write about the topic. Read the writing prompt. It gives your writing assignment.

Writing Prompt

Your school wants to buy one of the new kinds of lockers described in the article. Write a proposal recommending which kind of locker to buy and why. Use ideas from the article and at least one word from the Word Bank.

argument • influence • irritate • negotiate • stalemate

WRITING RUBRIC

In your response, you should:

- Write a proposal for the kind of locker you want.
- Use ideas from the article.
- Use at least one word from the Word Bank.
- Use correct grammar, usage, and mechanics.

Prewrite It

Once you are sure you understand the prompt, plan what you want to say.

1. Review the notes you made during the class discussion.

2. Reread the article. If there were points in your notes that you did not quite understand, clear them up now.

3. In the organizer on the right, make notes of your thoughts about the advantages of each kind of locker.

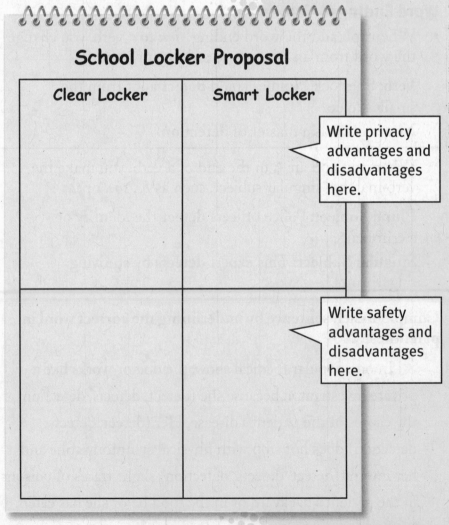

School Locker Proposal

Clear Locker	Smart Locker

Write privacy advantages and disadvantages here.

Write safety advantages and disadvantages here.

Draft It

Now use your organizer to draft, or write, a proposal for the locker you chose. The writing frame below will help you.

1. Start by naming the locker you want to propose.

2. Then give your reasons, first for privacy and then for safety. Finish each sentence starter by giving strong reasons for your suggestion. Make sure you explain your reasons with ideas from the article.

Sometimes, you do not really know your opinion about something until you talk about it. Talk with your partner about school lockers to help to form your opinion before you write.

Proposal

I propose that we buy (clear lockers, smart lockers). These would be good for privacy because _____

_____

_____

The lockers would also be good for safety because _____

_____

_____

_____

Check It and Fix It

After you have written your proposal, check your work. Try to read it with a "fresh eye." Imagine that you have never before read the proposal.

1. Is your proposal written clearly and correctly? The checklist on the right will help you see.

2. Trade proposals with a classmate. Talk about ways you both might improve your proposals. Use the ideas to revise your work.

3. For help with grammar, usage, and mechanics, go to the Handbook on pages 189–226.

✔ CHECKLIST

Evaluate your writing.
A score of "5" is excellent.
A score of "1" means you need to do more work.
Then ask a partner to rate your writing.

1. **Is the proposal clear?**
   Me: 1 2 3 4 5
   Partner: 1 2 3 4 5

2. **Is the proposal supported by reasons from the article?**
   Me: 1 2 3 4 5
   Partner: 1 2 3 4 5

3. **Is there at least one word from the Word Bank?**
   Me: 1 2 3 4 5
   Partner: 1 2 3 4 5

4. **Are grammar, usage, and mechanics correct?**
   Me: 1 2 3 4 5
   Partner: 1 2 3 4 5

Vocabulary Workshop

Add these words to your personal word bank by practicing them.

 **WORD BANK**

argument • influence • irritate • negotiate • stalemate

Your Choice

What other new words in the article would you like to remember? List them.

_____

_____

_____

Define It

Fill in the chart with the Word Bank words. In your own words, tell what each word means. Then circle the number that tells how well you understand each word. Circle "4" if you understand it completely. Circle "1" if you are not sure you understand the word at all. Use the example as a model.

What It Means	argument
a disagreement or fight	**How Well I Understand It** 1 2 3 ④
What It Means	
	How Well I Understand It 1 2 3 4
What It Means	
	How Well I Understand It 1 2 3 4
What It Means	
	How Well I Understand It 1 2 3 4
What It Means	
	How Well I Understand It 1 2 3 4

Show You Know

Write a dialogue, or conversation between people, in the space below. In your conversation, use all the Word Bank words in a way that shows you understand their meanings.

_____ : _____
          _____

_____ : _____
          _____

_____ : _____
          _____

_____ : _____
          _____

_____ : _____
          _____

_____ : _____
          _____

Partner Up

Trade dialogues with a partner. Choose roles and read each dialogue aloud. Did you use all the Word Bank words in your dialogue? Did you use the words correctly? Make revisions if you need to.

Word Sort

Fill in this chart with words from the Word Bank and the article. The chart is started for you.

Nouns	Verbs
stalemate	irritate

Now that you have sorted your words, pick two from different categories and use both in one sentence. For a challenge, use more than two of the words.

_____

_____

Write About It!

You have read an article about IQ testing. Now you will write about the topic. Read the writing prompt. It gives your writing assignment.

Writing Prompt

After reading "The IQ Question," what do you think students, teachers, and parents need to know about intelligence tests? Write a flyer to be handed out before testing begins at a school. Use ideas from the article and at least one word from the Word Bank.

insecurity • method • mislead • oppose • reaction

Prewrite It

Once you are sure you understand the prompt, plan what you want to say.

1. Review your notes from the class discussion. Use the organizer to start collecting your thoughts.

2. Reread the article. Look for more important points that need to be in your flyer. Add them to the organizer.

3. Take another look at all the points you have listed. Which are most important? Underline those points to use them in your flyer.

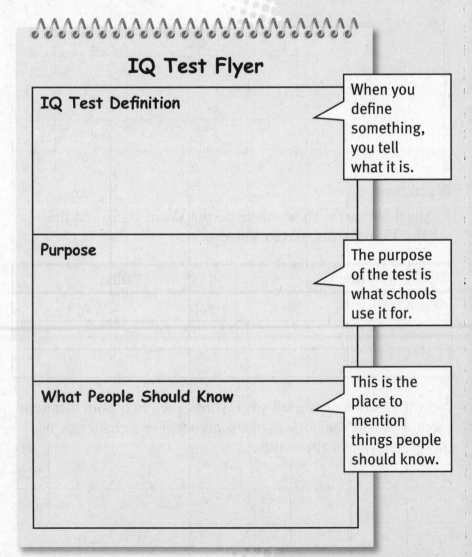

IQ Test Flyer

IQ Test Definition

When you define something, you tell what it is.

Purpose

The purpose of the test is what schools use it for.

What People Should Know

This is the place to mention things people should know.

Draft It

Now use your organizer to draft, or write, your flyer. The writing frame below will help you.

1. In each paragraph, finish the sentence starter by using ideas from your organizer.

2. Make sure you support your own thoughts on this subject by using ideas from the article.

Flyers commonly have bulleted points. Make the sentences for these points as short and clear as you can. A writing partner can help you get rid of unnecessary words.

What You Need to Know About IQ Tests

An IQ test is a special test that measures _____

_____

_____.

Schools use the test to _____

_____

_____.

Some facts you should know about the test are

• _____

• _____

• _____

Check It and Fix It

After you have written your flyer, check your work. Try to come to it fresh, as though you were reading it for the first time.

1. Is your flyer written clearly and correctly? The checklist on the right will help you see.

2. Trade flyers with a classmate. Talk about ways you both might improve your flyers. Use the ideas to revise your work.

3. For help with grammar, usage, and mechanics, go to the Handbook on pages 189–226.

✔ CHECKLIST

Evaluate your writing. A score of "5" is excellent. A score of "1" means you need to do more work. Then ask a partner to rate your writing.

1. Does the flyer state ideas clearly?

Me: 1 2 3 4 5
Partner: 1 2 3 4 5

2. Are there ideas from the article to support the main points?

Me: 1 2 3 4 5
Partner: 1 2 3 4 5

3. Is there at least one word from the Word Bank?

Me: 1 2 3 4 5
Partner: 1 2 3 4 5

4. Are grammar, usage, and mechanics correct?

Me: 1 2 3 4 5
Partner: 1 2 3 4 5

Vocabulary Workshop

Add these words to your personal word bank by practicing them.

WORD BANK insecurity • method • mislead • oppose • reaction

Your Choice

What other new words in the article would you like to remember? List them.

_____

_____

_____

Define It

For each organizer below, do as follows. Choose two words from the Word Bank and write them on either side of the triangle. (One word will appear twice.) On the blank "because" lines, tell why the two words are connected. Use the examples as a guide.

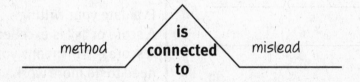

method — is connected to — mislead

because: if you used the wrong method for an experiment, the results could mislead you.

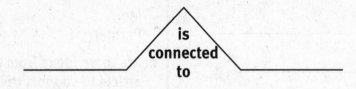

_____ — is connected to — _____

because: _____

_____

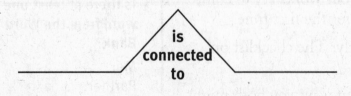

_____ — is connected to — _____

because: _____

_____

Word COACH

Try this game with a partner. Write a sentence for each Word Bank word. Then copy the sentences, leaving a blank where the Word Bank word goes. Challenge your partner to fill in each blank.

Show You Know

Answer the questions below to show you know the meaning of each Word Bank word. Explain each answer.

1. Would you feel **insecurity** about something you can do very well?

   _____

   _____

2. Would a **method** help you organize a work area? _____

   _____

   _____

3. Would you trust someone who often tried to **mislead** you? _____

   _____

4. Would you **oppose** a plan that you thought would work? _____

   _____

5. Would **laughter** be your reaction to a sad movie? _____

   _____

Partner Up

Trade answers with a partner. Discuss whether the answers are correct. Fix any mistakes.

Word Play

Using words with exact meanings can help you make your writing lively and specific. In the chart below, list words that mean the same or about the same as the Word Bank words. Think of words that have a precise meaning. Check a dictionary or thesaurus if you need to, and use the examples as models.

Word Bank Word	Words with Similar Meanings
method	system, technique, routine
insecurity	anxiety, shyness

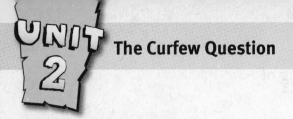

UNIT 2 The Curfew Question

Write About It!

You have read an article about teens and curfews. Now you will write about the topic. Read the writing prompt. It gives your writing assignment.

Writing Prompt

Imagine that your city is having a hearing about curfews. You have been invited to write and deliver a short speech giving your opinion about what curfews accomplish. Use ideas from the article and at least one word from the Word Bank.

cause • oppose • reaction • solution • violence

Prewrite It

Once you are sure you understand the prompt, plan what you want to say.

1. Review your notes from the class discussion. Use the organizer to start listing effects of youth curfews.

2. Reread the article. Continue to add ideas to the organizer.

3. Take another look at all the points you have listed. Which are the strongest? Cross out the points that are not as strong. Decide what is most important to put in your speech.

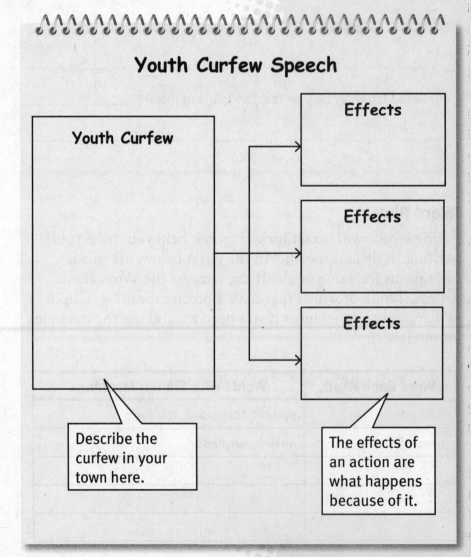

Youth Curfew Speech

Youth Curfew

Effects

Effects

Effects

Describe the curfew in your town here.

The effects of an action are what happens because of it.

Draft It

Now use your organizer to draft, or write, your speech. The writing frame below will help you.

1. Start by giving your opinion. You have two choices, either for or against. Underline your choice.

2. Support your opinion with reasons. Make sure you explain your reasons with ideas and examples from the article.

Curfew Recommendations

Good afternoon and thank you for inviting me to speak.

I believe that this city (should, should not) have a curfew.

The effects of a curfew are _____

_____

_____

_____

_____

_____

_____

_____.

Check It and Fix It

After you have written your speech, check your work. Try to read it with a "fresh eye." Imagine that you are listening to this speech and trying to make a decision.

1. Is your speech written clearly and correctly? The checklist on the right will help you figure that out.

2. Deliver your speech to a classmate and then listen to his or hers. Talk about ways you both might improve your speeches. Use the ideas to revise your work.

3. For help with grammar, usage, and mechanics, go to the Handbook on pages 189–226.

✔ **CHECKLIST**

Evaluate your writing. A score of "5" is excellent. A score of "1" means you need to do more work. Then ask a partner to rate your writing.

1. **Does the speech state reasons clearly?**

   Me: 1 2 3 4 5
   Partner: 1 2 3 4 5

2. **Is there information from the article?**

   Me: 1 2 3 4 5
   Partner: 1 2 3 4 5

3. **Is there at least one word from the Word Bank?**

   Me: 1 2 3 4 5
   Partner: 1 2 3 4 5

4. **Are grammar, usage, and mechanics correct?**

   Me: 1 2 3 4 5
   Partner: 1 2 3 4 5

Vocabulary Workshop

Add these words to your personal word bank by practicing them.

WORD BANK cause • oppose • reaction • solution • violence

Define It

Complete the chart below using the Word Bank words. First, tell what the word means. Then tell what the word does not mean. Use the example as a guide.

Word	What It Is	What It Is Not
cause	a reason for something	an effect

Show You Know

Answer the questions below to show you know the meaning of each Word Bank word. Explain each answer.

1. Could icy sidewalks **cause** you to fall? _____

   _____

2. Would most ballplayers **oppose** cheering at a game? _____

   _____

3. What would a sports crowd's **reaction** be to a win? _____

   _____

4. Does every problem have a **solution**? _____

   _____

5. Is hitting someone a form of **violence**? _____

   _____

Partner Up

Trade answers with a classmate. Are his or her answers similar to yours? If not, talk over who is right. Fix any mistakes.

Word Sort

Fill in the chart below with words from the Word Bank and the article. The chart is started for you.

Words with Suffixes	Words Without Suffixes
reaction	cause

Now that you have sorted your words, pick two from different categories and use both in one sentence. For a challenge, use more than two of the words.

_____

_____

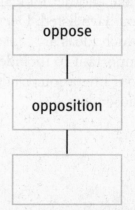

ALL IN THE FAMILY

The following words are in the same word family. What other words have a form of *oppose* in them? Add one to the list.

oppose

opposition

[ ]

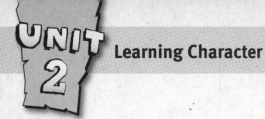

UNIT 2 — Learning Character

Write About It!

You have read an article about character education. Now you will write about the topic. Read the writing prompt. It gives your writing assignment.

Writing Prompt

After reading "Learning Character," who do you think should be involved in teaching kids about character? Write an invitation to parents to attend a meeting to plan a character learning course. Use ideas from the article and at least one word from the Word Bank.

argument • interact • introduce • victorious • viewpoint

Prewrite It

Once you are sure you understand the prompt, plan what you want to say.

1. Review your notes from the class discussion. Use your notes to start filling in the organizer.

2. Reread the article. Use information from the article to add details to the organizer.

3. Take another look at what you have listed. Decide which ideas are most important to include in your invitation. Underline those ideas.

Character Learning

Who should decide if it is taught?	Reasons it might be good for our school:	Reasons it might not be good for our school:

Draft It

Now use your organizer to draft, or write, your invitation. The writing frame below will help you.

1. In each paragraph, start by stating your opinion. Underline the choice that expresses your view. (In the first paragraph, you may underline more than one choice.)

2. Then give your reasons. Finish the thought in each paragraph by giving strong reasons for your opinion. Make sure you explain your reasons with ideas from the article.

Dear Parents:

Please come to a meeting to talk about a course on

learning character. (Parents, teachers, students) should be

involved in this decision because _____

_____

_____

_____.

A course like this one (would, would not) be good for our

school because _____

_____

_____

_____.

Check It and Fix It

After you have written your invitation, check your work. Try to read it with a "fresh eye." Imagine that you have never before read the invitation.

1. Is the invitation clear and correct? The checklist on the right will help you see.

2. Trade invitations with a classmate. Talk about ways you both might improve your invitations. Revise your work if you think revisions are necessary.

3. For help with grammar, usage, and mechanics, go to the Handbook on pages 189–226.

Writing COACH

If you run into trouble while you are writing, stop and talk with a partner. The conversation might help you get the ideas flowing again.

✔ CHECKLIST

Evaluate your writing. A score of "5" is excellent. A score of "1" means you need to do more work. Then ask a partner to rate your writing.

1. **Does the invitation clearly tell parents why they should attend the meeting?**

   Me: 1 2 3 4 5
   Partner: 1 2 3 4 5

2. **Are there ideas from the article to support the points?**

   Me: 1 2 3 4 5
   Partner: 1 2 3 4 5

3. **Is there at least one word from the Word Bank?**

   Me: 1 2 3 4 5
   Partner: 1 2 3 4 5

4. **Are grammar, usage, and mechanics correct?**

   Me: 1 2 3 4 5
   Partner: 1 2 3 4 5

Vocabulary Workshop

Add these words to your personal word bank by practicing them.

WORD BANK argument • interact • introduce • victorious • viewpoint

Your Choice

What other new words in the article would you like to remember? List them.

_____

_____

_____

Define It

Complete the chart below using the Word Bank words. First, tell what the word means. Then tell what the word does not mean.

Word	What It Is	What It Is Not

Show You Know

To show that you understand the Word Bank words, write a clue for each word. Exchange clues with a partner. See whether your partner can identify the correct word for each clue.

1. _____

2. _____

3. _____

4. _____

5. _____

Word Play

Using words with exact meanings can help you make your writing more lively and specific. In the chart below, list words that mean the same or about the same as the Word Bank words. Think of words that have a precise meaning. Check a dictionary or thesaurus if you need to, and use the examples as models.

Word Bank Word	Words with Similar Meanings
argument	quarrel, disagreement
interact	cooperate, relate

Now try some of the words to see how they can make your writing more precise. Rewrite each of the sentences below, substituting one of your words for the boldface word.

1. My brother and I had an **argument** over chores.

_____

2. It is important for teammates to **interact**.

_____

Writing Reflection

 Can all conflicts be resolved?

Look through your writing from this unit and choose the best piece. Reflect on this piece of writing by completing each sentence below.

My best piece of writing from this unit is _____

_____

I chose this piece because _____

_____

_____

While I was writing, one goal I had was _____

_____

I accomplished this goal by _____

_____

_____

This writing helped me think more about the Big Question because

_____

_____

One thing I learned while writing that can help me in the future is

_____

_____

 How much information is enough?

Kids Just Want to Have Fun
Write About It! Advice Column 70
Vocabulary Workshop 72

Righteous Heroes
Write About It! Feature Story 74
Vocabulary Workshop 76

The People's Art
Write About It! Memo 78
Vocabulary Workshop 80

Someone to Look Up To
Write About It! Thank-You Note 82
Vocabulary Workshop 84

Net Smarts
Write About It! List of Tips 86
Vocabulary Workshop 88

Old Enough to Vote?
Write About It! Speech 90
Vocabulary Workshop 92

Help Yourself and Others
Write About It! Editorial 94
Vocabulary Workshop 96

Too Much Information!
Write About It! Essay 98
Vocabulary Workshop 100

Write About It!

You have read an article about parents' involvement in organized sports. Now you will write about the topic. Read the writing prompt. It gives your writing assignment.

Writing Prompt

After reading "Kids Just Want to Have Fun," in what ways do you think parents should be involved in their kids' sports? Imagine that you are an expert on the issue. Write an advice column to parents whose children want to join a sports team. Use ideas from the article and at least one word from the Word Bank.

challenge • decision • development • locate • valuable

In your response, you should:

- Write an advice column to parents about kids in sports.

- Give guidelines on what parents should and should not do.

- Use at least one word from the Word Bank.

- Use correct grammar, usage, and mechanics.

Prewrite It

Once you are sure you understand the prompt, plan what you want to say.

1. Look over your notes from the class discussion. Fill in the organizer on the right with information from your notes.

2. Reread the article. Look for additional Do's and Don'ts for parents. Add those to your organizer.

3. Take another look at your organizer. Cross out or change points that are weaker than others.

Advice to Parents

Do's	Don'ts

The Do's are things parents can do to help kids who play sports.

The Don'ts are things parents should *not* do.

Draft It

Now use your organizer to draft, or write, your advice column. The writing frame below will help you.

1. Start by giving one piece of advice.

2. Include the Do and the Don't points that you added to your organizer. Make sure you use information and ideas from the article. Add examples to make your points clearer.

Work with a partner to write a better column. Ask, Is my advice clear? Is it respectful? Discuss specific ways you can improve your advice. Write them down; then revise your column.

Advice to Sports Parents

Parents, here are some things you can do to help your kids

get the most out of playing sports. First, _____

_____

_____

_____

_____

_____

_____

_____

_____

_____ .

Check It and Fix It

After you have written your advice column, check your work. Try to read it as a parent who needs advice on what to do. How can your information help that person?

1. Is everything written clearly and correctly? Use the checklist on the right to decide.

2. Trade columns with a classmate. Discuss ways you both might improve your columns. Then use ideas from your discussion to revise your work.

3. For help with grammar, usage, and mechanics, go to the Handbook on pages 189–226.

✔ CHECKLIST

Evaluate your writing. A score of "5" is excellent. A score of "1" means you need to do more work. Then ask a partner to rate your writing.

1. **Does the column give parents good advice?**

   Me: 1 2 3 4 5
   Partner: 1 2 3 4 5

2. **Does the column include details from the article?**

   Me: 1 2 3 4 5
   Partner: 1 2 3 4 5

3. **Is there at least one word from the Word Bank?**

   Me: 1 2 3 4 5
   Partner: 1 2 3 4 5

4. **Are grammar, usage, and mechanics correct?**

   Me: 1 2 3 4 5
   Partner: 1 2 3 4 5

Vocabulary Workshop

Add these words to your personal word bank by practicing them.

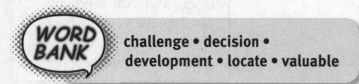

WORD BANK challenge • decision • development • locate • valuable

Your Choice

What other new words in the article would you like to remember? List them.

_____

_____

_____

Define It

Complete the chart below. In the first column, write each word in the Word Bank. In the second column, write the meaning of each word. In the last column, write clues from the article that help you understand the word's meaning. The first row is done for you as a guide.

Word	What It Means	Clues from Text
challenge	say someone is or might be wrong	forget good sportsmanship, argue with officials

Show You Know

In the space below, write a short, short story (just a paragraph!) using the Word Bank words. Be sure your sentences show that you know the meanings of the words.

Once upon a time, _____

_____

_____

_____

_____

_____

_____

_____

Partner Up

Read your story to a partner. Did you use all the Word Bank words, and did you use them correctly? If not, ask your partner for help.

Word Endings: -able

- The word ending -*able* means "to be worthy of" or "to be capable." The ending -*able* changes an action (verb) or a thing (noun) into a describing word (adjective).

   Verb: Riko and I **value** Hector's company.

   Noun: You really cannot put a **value** on friendship.

   Adjective: Friendship is a **valuable** thing.

Complete each sentence by underlining the correct word in parentheses.

My father wanted to buy a new, more (value, valuable) automobile. Before he bought it, he looked on the Internet to find out the (value, valuable) of his old car. He was surprised by his old car's (value, valuable). In fact, that made him (value, valuable) the old car so much that he decided to keep it for a while!

ALL IN THE FAMILY

The words below belong to the same word family. What other words have the word *value* in them? Add one to the list.

value

valuable

UNIT 3

Righteous Heroes

Write About It!

You have read an article about heroes who helped save lives during World War II. Now you will write about the topic. Read the writing prompt. It gives your writing assignment.

Writing Prompt

Suppose you work for a newspaper that plans to run a series on past heroes. Write a feature story on Oskar Schindler that answers *Who? What? Where? When? Why?* and *How?* Use information from the article and at least one word from the Word Bank.

discrimination • global • inequality • invariably • statistics

WRITING RUBRIC

In your response, you should:

- Write a feature newspaper story about Oskar Schindler.

- Include information from the article answering *Who? What? Where? When? Why?* and *How?*

- Use at least one word from the Word Bank.

- Use correct grammar, usage, and mechanics.

Prewrite It

Once you are sure you understand the prompt, plan what you want to say.

1. Review your notes from the class discussion. Jot down important ideas on the organizer.

2. Reread the article. Look for additional points about Schindler. Add those to your organizer.

3. Take another look at your organizer. If you need to revise your points, make the changes.

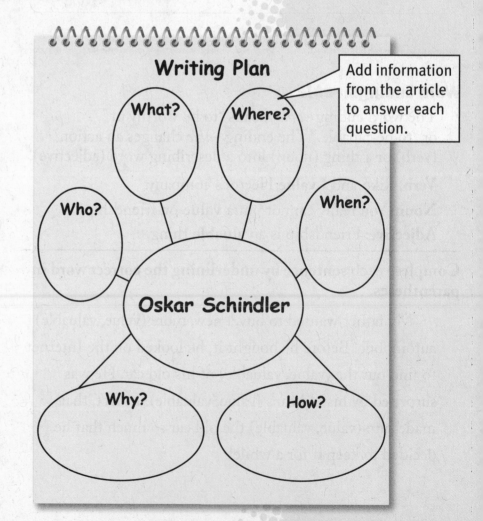

Writing Plan

Add information from the article to answer each question.

What?
Where?
Who?
When?
Oskar Schindler
Why?
How?

Draft It

Now use your organizer to draft, or write, your feature story. The writing frame below will help you.

1. Complete the first sentence by giving one reason that Oskar Schindler is considered a hero.

2. Give facts about Schindler based on points you added to your organizer. Then go on to explain how Schindler helped people and why he is considered a hero. Make sure you use information and ideas from the article.

If you have trouble organizing your feature or expressing your points, work with a partner. Read each sentence aloud to see what your partner understood or what might have been confusing.

▌ THIS JUST IN ▌

Oskar Schindler: Hero

Oskar Schindler is considered a righteous hero because

_____

_____

_____

_____

_____

_____

_____

_____

_____ .

Check It and Fix It

After you have written your feature story, check your work. Try to read it as someone who has just picked up the newspaper and knows nothing about Oskar Schindler.

1. Is everything written clearly and correctly? Use the checklist on the right to decide.

2. Trade stories with a classmate. Talk over ways you both might improve your stories. Then use ideas from your discussion to revise your work.

3. For help with grammar, usage, and mechanics, go to the Handbook on pages 189–226.

✔ CHECKLIST

Evaluate your writing. A score of "5" is excellent. A score of "1" means you need to do more work. Then ask a partner to rate your writing.

1. **Does the feature explain clearly why Schindler was a hero?**

   Me: 1 2 3 4 5
   Partner: 1 2 3 4 5

2. **Does the feature contain information from the article?**

   Me: 1 2 3 4 5
   Partner: 1 2 3 4 5

3. **Is there at least one word from the Word Bank?**

   Me: 1 2 3 4 5
   Partner: 1 2 3 4 5

4. **Are grammar, usage, and mechanics correct?**

   Me: 1 2 3 4 5
   Partner: 1 2 3 4 5

Vocabulary Workshop

Add these words to your personal word bank by practicing them.

WORD BANK discrimination • global • inequality • invariably • statistics

What other new words in the article would you like to remember? List them.

_____

_____

_____

Define It

For each set of boxes below, do as follows. Choose two words from the Word Bank and write them in the small boxes. (One word will appear twice.) In the Connection box, describe how the two are connected. Use the example as a guide.

| statistics | and | invariably |

Connection:
Statistics are not invariably right. They can be wrong.

Word COACH

Understanding how words are connected can help you use them correctly. Try to connect new words in your writing and speaking.

| | and | |

Connection:

| | and | |

Connection:

Show You Know

To show that you understand the Word Bank words, write three sentences. In each sentence, use and highlight two of the words. (You will use one word twice.) Use the example as a model.

- Because discrimination happens in many countries, it is a global problem. _____

1. _____

   _____

2. _____

   _____

3. _____

   _____

Partner Up

Trade sentences with a partner. Check each other's sentences. If something is unclear or incorrect, talk over how to fix it. Then make corrections.

Combining Forms: *equi-*

- The combining form *equi-* comes from a Latin word that means "equal." Words combined with *equi-* (or *equ-*) all contain the meaning "equal."

  Equator: The equator is an imaginary line around the globe that divides it into equal halves.

  Equidistant: A midpoint is equidistant, or halfway, from the beginning and the end.

  Equation: An equation shows that the two sides of a math operation are equal.

Complete each sentence by underlining the correct word in parentheses.

My geography teacher taught us about the Earth's (equator, equidistant, equation). She said that it is (equator, equidistant, equation) from the North Pole and the South Pole. I wonder what kind of (equator, equidistant, equation) a math expert used to figure that out!

The words below all belong to the same word family. Circle those that appear in the article.

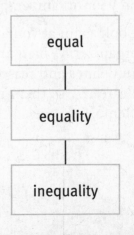

equal

equality

inequality

Write About It!

You have read an article about selecting and displaying art in public places. Now you will write about the topic. Read the writing prompt. It gives your writing assignment.

Writing Prompt

After reading "The People's Art," who do you think should choose the kind of artwork shown in public places? Suppose your school wants to exhibit a piece of art outside. Write a memo to the school board with guidelines on the type of art to be bought and on who gets to decide. Use ideas from the article and at least one word from the Word Bank.

criteria • decision • exploration • quality • quantity

WRITING RUBRIC

In your response, you should:

- Write a memo to the school board with guidelines on what art to buy and who should choose it.

- Include ideas from the article.

- Use at least one word from the Word Bank.

- Use correct grammar, usage, and mechanics.

Prewrite It

Once you are sure you understand the prompt, plan what you want to say.

1. Look over notes from your class discussion. Start writing your ideas on the organizer on the right.

2. Reread the article. Which ideas might become guidelines? Write them on your organizer.

3. Look again at your organizer. Which guidelines and reasons are clearest? Use them in your memo.

Who Decides?	Why?
1.	1.
2.	2.
3.	3.

Guidelines for Type of Art to Choose
1.
2.
3.
4.
5.

Draft It

Now use your organizer to draft, or write, your memo to the school board. The writing frame below will help you.

1. Start by telling who should choose the art. Underline the choices you agree with. Explain why.

2. Review concerns and criteria mentioned in the article and make sure your guidelines address them.

A partner can help you write a better memo. Ask a partner to read each sentence to see if the guidelines are clear. Are the reasons persuasive? If not, discuss ways to improve them.

TO: Members of the School Board

The new public art at our school should be

chosen by the (students, teachers, parents,

community) because _____

_____

_____

_____.

Guidelines for type of art to buy: _____

_____

_____

_____

_____.

✔ **CHECKLIST**

Evaluate your writing. A score of "5" is excellent. A score of "1" means you need to do more work. Then ask a partner to rate your writing.

1. **Does the memo give clear guidelines?**

   Me: 1 2 3 4 5
   Partner: 1 2 3 4 5

2. **Does the memo include information from the article?**

   Me: 1 2 3 4 5
   Partner: 1 2 3 4 5

3. **Is there at least one word from the Word Bank?**

   Me: 1 2 3 4 5
   Partner: 1 2 3 4 5

4. **Are grammar, usage, and mechanics correct?**

   Me: 1 2 3 4 5
   Partner: 1 2 3 4 5

Check It and Fix It

After you have written your memo, check your work. Read it as if you are a member of the school board. Do the guidelines make sense to you?

1. Is everything written clearly and correctly? Use the checklist on the right to decide.

2. Trade memos with a classmate. Discuss ways you and your partner might improve your memos. Use each other's comments to make changes.

3. For help with grammar, usage, and mechanics, go to the Handbook on pages 189–226.

Vocabulary Workshop

Add these words to your personal word bank by practicing them.

criteria • decision • exploration • quality • quantity

Your Choice

What other new words in the article would you like to remember? List them.

_____

_____

_____

Define It

Complete Venn diagrams to show how words are different and alike. Choose a pair of words from the Word Bank. Write the words on the lines inside each circle. On the sides of the circles, tell how the two words are different. In between, write how they are similar. Do this for three pairs of words. You will use one word twice.

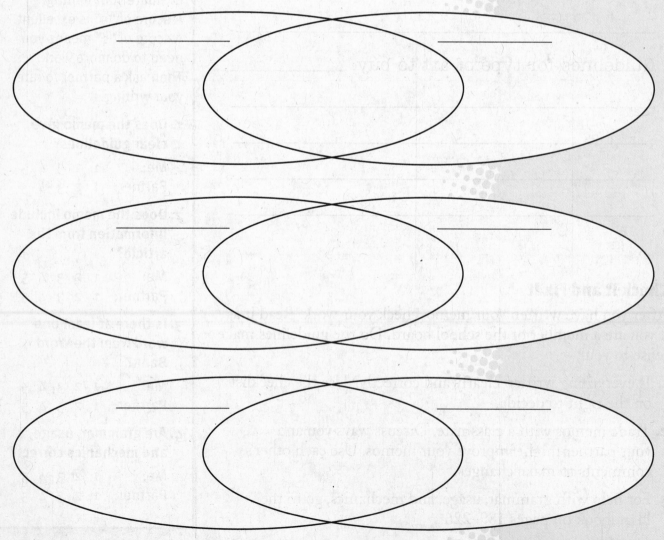

Show You Know

Write a dialogue, or conversation between people, in the space below. In your conversation, use all the Word Bank words in a way that shows you understand their meanings.

_____ : _____

_____

_____ : _____

_____

_____ : _____

_____

_____ : _____

_____

Partner Up

Read your dialogue aloud with a partner. Each of you can read a different part. If something is unclear, talk over how to fix it. Then make the corrections.

Word Endings: *-ty, -ity*

- When you add the word ending *-ty* or *-ity* to a describing word, or adjective, you change the adjective into a noun. For example, the adjective *quantum* means "large or significant." If you add *-ity* to the base of the word, you form *quantity,* a noun meaning "amount."

Adjective: When the factory made twice as many goods, production took a **quantum** leap.

Noun: Experts studied how they increased the **quantity** of goods produced.

Complete each sentence by underlining the correct word in parentheses.

Many kings and queens of old were members of ancient (royal, royalty) families. When one died, he or she was usually replaced by other (royal, royalty). A king's and queen's (loyal, loyalty) subjects showed their (loyal, loyalty) by giving gifts and bowing. If (cruel, cruelty) kings or queens distrusted their subjects, they might put them in dungeons or carry out other forms of (cruel, cruelty).

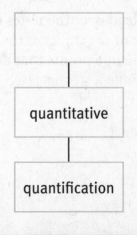

The words below are in the same word family. What word in this family can you find in the article? Write it in the first box.

quantitative

quantification

The People's Art   **81**

WRITING RUBRIC

Write About It!

You have read an article about what makes a good role model. Now you will write about the topic. Read the writing prompt. It gives your writing assignment.

Writing Prompt

After reading "Someone to Look Up To," do you know what makes a good role model? Write a thank-you note to someone who has been a good role model to you. Use ideas from the article and at least one word from the Word Bank.

discrimination • explanation • factor • point • reveal

In your response, you should:

- Write a thank-you note to a person who is your role model.
- Use details from the article as well as from your experiences.
- Use at least one word from the Word Bank.
- Use correct grammar, usage, and mechanics.

Prewrite It

Once you are sure you understand the prompt, plan what you want to say.

1. Look over notes from the class discussion. Begin filling in the organizer on the right.

2. Reread the article to see if there are any other qualities you might include on your organizer.

3. Read over the notes on your organizer. Cross out or change points that do not make a strong case.

Quality: _____

Lesson or Memory:

_____

_____

_____

_____

_____

_____

_____

Quality: _____

Quality: _____

The qualities describe what makes the person a good role model.

The lesson or memory tells what you learned from your role model.

Draft It

Now use your organizer to draft, or write, your thank-you note. The writing frame below will help you.

1. Start by giving the name of your role model. Then complete the first sentence. Continue by recalling a memory in which you learned a valuable lesson from your role model.

2. Review qualities you included in your organizer. Explain how those make your role model someone to look up to.

Dear _____,

   You may not know it, but thanks to you _____

_____

_____

_____

_____

_____

_____

_____

_____

_____ .

Check It and Fix It

After you have written your thank-you note, check your work. Read it as if you were the role model receiving the note.

1. Is everything written clearly and correctly? Use the checklist on the right to decide.

2. Trade notes with a classmate. Read each other's thank-you notes and discuss ways you both might improve them. Then use ideas from your discussion to revise your work.

3. For help with grammar, usage, and mechanics, go to the Handbook on pages 189–226.

> **To improve your thank-you note, work with a partner. Ask, Can you clearly picture my role model and why I look up to him or her? Use good suggestions from your partner to revise your note.**

✔ CHECKLIST

Evaluate your writing. A score of "5" is excellent. A score of "1" means you need to do more work. Then ask a partner to rate your writing.

1. **Does the note explain why the person is a good role model?**

   Me: 1 2 3 4 5
   Partner: 1 2 3 4 5

2. **Does the note include ideas from the article?**

   Me: 1 2 3 4 5
   Partner: 1 2 3 4 5

3. **Is there at least one word from the Word Bank?**

   Me: 1 2 3 4 5
   Partner: 1 2 3 4 5

4. **Are grammar, usage, and mechanics correct?**

   Me: 1 2 3 4 5
   Partner: 1 2 3 4 5

Vocabulary Workshop

Add these words to your personal word bank by practicing them.

WORD BANK

discrimination • explanation • factor • point • reveal

Your Choice

What other new words in the article would you like to remember? List them.

_____

_____

_____

Define It

For each organizer below, do as follows. Choose two words from the Word Bank and write them on either side of the triangle. (One word will appear twice.) On the blank "because" lines, tell why the two words are connected. Use the example as a guide.

discrimination   **is connected to**   reveal

_____

because: discrimination is something people do not want to reveal. _____

_____

_____   **is connected to**   _____

because: _____

_____

_____   **is connected to**   _____

because: _____

_____

Show You Know

Answer the questions below to show you know the meaning of each Word Bank word.

1. How could **discrimination** in some schools lead the government to enact new fairness laws?

   _____

2. Would you be able to have an **explanation** for a mysterious letter in the mail? Why?

   _____

3. What might be a **factor** in deciding what to make for dinner?

   _____

4. You made such a good **point** in the debate, no one could argue. What did you do?

   _____

5. What might you do so that you do not **reveal** a secret?

   _____

Partner Up

Take turns with a partner reading the questions and answering them. Do the answers show an understanding of the Word Bank words? If not, work with your partner to rewrite them.

Multiple-Meaning Words

Some words have more than one meaning. For example, *point* can mean "an idea or fact" or "a dot." Both meanings of *point* are nouns, but *point* can also be a verb meaning "to direct or to show." Here are two meanings for the word *factor*: **(a) factor** *noun* a cause or happening that helps bring about a result; **(b) factor** *noun* any of the numbers that can be multiplied together to form a product.

Which meaning of *factor*—(a) or (b)—makes sense in the following sentence? Write the letter here: _____.

• The numbers 2 and 5 are two factors of 10.

UNIT 3 **Net Smarts**

Write About It!

You have read an article about researching on the Internet. Now you will write about the topic. Read the writing prompt. It gives your writing assignment.

WRITING RUBRIC

In your response, you should:

- Write a list of Do's and Don'ts for finding reliable Web sites.

- Include in your list some of the tips from the article.

- Use at least one word from the Word Bank.

- Use correct grammar, usage, and mechanics.

Writing Prompt

After reading "Net Smarts," do you know which kind of Web sites you can trust and which you cannot? Help inform other students. Write a list of Do's and Don'ts for surfing the Web that you could post in your school library. Use ideas from the article and at least one word from the Word Bank.

exploration • quality • quantity • statistics

Prewrite It

Once you are sure you understand the prompt, plan what you want to say.

1. Look over notes from the class discussion. Fill in the organizer on the right with items you might want to put on your list.

2. Reread the article to see what advice was given. Which tips were Do's, and which cautions were Don'ts? Add them to your organizer.

3. Look again at your organizer. If you can think of additional tips or cautions, add them.

Finding Reliable Web Sites

Do's	Don'ts

Draft It

Now use your organizer to draft, or write, your list. The writing frame below will help you.

1. Start by filling in the first sentence.

2. Then use your organizer to write out and explain each piece of advice (Do's) and each warning (Don'ts). Be sure to include information given in the article.

A partner can help you tell if your list is clear. Do the Do's and Don'ts give helpful tips? If not, discuss how to make the list more informative.

Search for Sure!

These Do's and Don'ts can help you _____

_____

_____

_____ .

Do's: _____

_____

_____

Don'ts: _____

_____

_____

✔ **CHECKLIST**

Evaluate your writing. A score of "5" is excellent. A score of "1" means you need to do more work. Then ask a partner to rate your writing.

1. Does the list give clear advice and warnings?

Me: 1 2 3 4 5
Partner: 1 2 3 4 5

2. Do the Do's and Don'ts include advice from the article?

Me: 1 2 3 4 5
Partner: 1 2 3 4 5

3. Is there at least one word from the Word Bank?

Me: 1 2 3 4 5
Partner: 1 2 3 4 5

4. Are grammar, usage, and mechanics correct?

Me: 1 2 3 4 5
Partner: 1 2 3 4 5

Check It and Fix It

After you have written your list, check your work. Imagine that it is hanging on a wall in your school library. Does it give good advice?

1. Is everything written clearly and correctly? Use the checklist on the right to decide.

2. Exchange lists with a partner. Are the Do's and Don'ts clear and helpful? Discuss ways you might improve your lists. Use your partner's comments to make changes.

3. For help with grammar, usage, and mechanics, go to the Handbook on pages 189–226.

Vocabulary Workshop

Add these words to your personal word bank by practicing them.

exploration • quality • quantity • statistics

Define It

For each organizer below, do as follows. Choose two words from the Word Bank and write them on either side of the triangle. On the blank "because" lines, tell why the two words are connected.

is connected to

because: _____
_____

is connected to

because: _____
_____

Your Choice

What other new words in the article would you like to remember? List them.

_____
_____
_____

Word COACH

When you understand how words are connected, you can use them in meaningful ways. Using new words together in sentences will help you remember them.

Show You Know

Answer the questions below to show you know the meaning of each Word Bank word.

1. Why might some **exploration** be dangerous?
   _____

2. If your boss wants to talk to you about the good **quality** of your work, should you be concerned about your job? Explain.
   _____

3. In what subjects in school do you talk about **quantity**?
   _____

4. What is something that can be proven with **statistics**?
   _____

Partner Up

Take turns with a partner reading the questions and answering them. Do the answers show you understand the Word Bank words? If not, work with your partner to rewrite them.

Word Play

Using words with exact meanings can make your writing more lively and specific. In the chart below, list some words that mean the same or about the same as the Word Bank words. Think of words that have a precise meaning. Check a dictionary or thesaurus if you need to, and use the examples as models.

Word Bank Word	Words with Similar Meanings
exploration	searching, investigation
quantity	amount, number

UNIT 3

Old Enough to Vote?

WRITING RUBRIC

Write About It!

You have read an article about possibly lowering the U.S. voting age to sixteen. Now you will write about the topic. Read the writing prompt. It gives your writing assignment.

In your response, you should:

- Write a speech for or against sixteen-year-olds voting in the U.S.

- Include ideas from the article.

- Use at least one word from the Word Bank.

- Use correct grammar, usage, and mechanics.

Writing Prompt

Do you think sixteen-year-olds should be able to vote? Imagine that the parent-teacher group at your school has organized a "Speak Out" event. Write a speech to deliver to parents. Argue either for or against the issue. Use ideas from the article and at least one word from the Word Bank.

accumulate • derive • global • inequality

Prewrite It

Once you are sure you understand the prompt, plan what you want to say.

1. Look over notes from the class discussion. Can you use any ideas in your speech? Jot them down on the organizer on the right.

2. Reread the article to see what arguments each side uses. Which ones do you agree with? Add them to your organizer.

3. Read through the arguments on your organizer. Make sure they present a good case. If not, add stronger arguments.

The Voting Age Debate

My Opinion

_____

_____

> Your opinion is for or against lowering the U.S. voting age.

My Arguments

_____

_____

_____

_____

_____

_____

_____

> Your arguments explain why you feel that way.

Draft It

Now use your organizer to draft, or write, your speech to parents. The writing frame below will help you.

1. Start by underlining your opinion. Then continue to write your speech by explaining your reasons or arguments.

2. Review the arguments you jotted down on your organizer. Be sure to include those and any other reasons you may have.

Delivering your speech to a real audience can help you discover whether it is clear and convincing. Ask a partner to listen and respond.

Opinion Speech

Good Evening, Ladies and Gentlemen.

Should sixteen-year-olds be allowed to vote in the U.S.?

It is my firm belief that they (should, should not).

Here are my reasons: _____

_____

_____

_____

_____

_____

_____ .

✔ CHECKLIST

Evaluate your writing. A score of "5" is excellent. A score of "1" means you need to do more work. Then ask a partner to rate your writing.

1. **Does the speech present views clearly and convincingly?**

   Me: 1 2 3 4 5
   Partner: 1 2 3 4 5

2. **Does the speech include points mentioned in the article?**

   Me: 1 2 3 4 5
   Partner: 1 2 3 4 5

3. **Is there at least one word from the Word Bank?**

   Me: 1 2 3 4 5
   Partner: 1 2 3 4 5

4. **Are grammar, usage, and mechanics correct?**

   Me: 1 2 3 4 5
   Partner: 1 2 3 4 5

Check It and Fix It

After you have written your speech, check your work. Read it aloud as though you are delivering it.

1. Is everything written clearly and correctly? Use the checklist on the right to decide.

2. Ask a classmate to listen to your speech. Then listen to your partner's speech. Discuss ways you both might improve your work. Use each other's comments to make changes.

3. For help with grammar, usage, and mechanics, go to the Handbook on pages 189–226.

Vocabulary Workshop

Add these words to your personal word bank by practicing them.

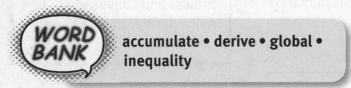

WORD BANK accumulate • derive • global • inequality

Your Choice

What other new words in the article would you like to remember? List them.

_____

_____

_____

Define It

Complete the chart below using each word from the Word Bank. Give the meaning in your own words. Then write a real-life example and an example that connects to your life. Use the sample answers on the chart as a guide.

Word	Real-Life Example	My Connection
accumulate: get bigger piece by piece	The weather report said that snow might accumulate up to three inches.	I get stressed out if I accumulate too much homework.

Show You Know

To show that you understand the Word Bank words, write a clue for each word. Exchange clues with a partner. See whether your partner can identify the correct word for each clue. Use the clue for the word *global*, below, as a model.

• This is something that happens beyond our own community.

1. _____

2. _____

3. _____

4. _____

Partner Up

Take turns reading clue sentences and seeing if your partner can guess the words. If a sentence is unclear, talk about how to make it clearer. Then make the necessary changes.

Word Endings: *-al*

• When you add the word ending *-al* to a noun, you change the word into an adjective, or describing word.

Noun: People in almost every country around the **globe** struggle with poverty and disease.
Adjective: Health care is a **global** issue.

Complete each sentence below by underlining the correct word in parentheses.

The circus performer amazed the crowd with her (magic, magical). Each feat was more (magic, magical) than the one before. When she pulled the three little ducks out of her hat, they made a strange and (comic, comical) quacking sound. Everyone expected the magician to pull out rabbits and did not expect her to be such a (comic, comical). Even her (music, musical) talent made us laugh. She played her (music, musical) on a giant kazoo!

The words below are all part of the same word family. Which ones appear in the article you read? Circle them.

globe

global

globally

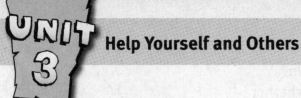

UNIT 3 — Help Yourself and Others

Write About It!

You have read an article about whether schools and states should require young people to volunteer. Now you will write about the topic. Read the writing prompt. It gives your writing assignment.

Writing Prompt

After reading "Help Yourself and Others," do you believe that teens should be required to do volunteer work? Write an editorial for your school paper in which you give your opinion. Use ideas from the article and at least one word from the Word Bank.

challenge • development • exploration • valuable

WRITING RUBRIC

In your response, you should:

- Write an editorial giving your opinion on volunteering.

- Include ideas from the article to support your opinion.

- Use at least one word from the Word Bank.

- Use correct grammar, usage, and mechanics.

Prewrite It

Once you are sure you understand the prompt, plan what you want to say.

1. Look over notes from the class discussion. In the center of the organizer on the right, underline your opinion.

2. Reread the article to look for ideas you might use in your article. Add them to the organizer.

3. Look again at your organizer. Add any other reasons you feel strongly about.

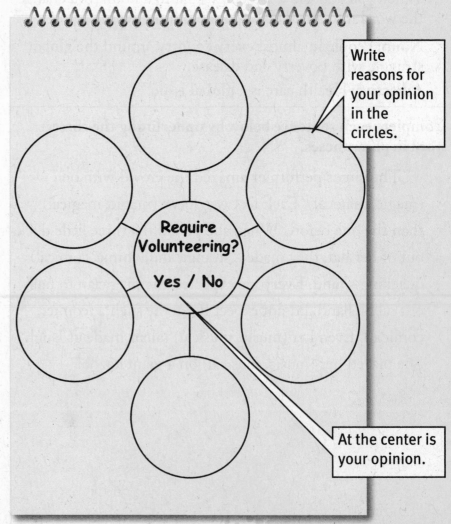

Write reasons for your opinion in the circles.

Require Volunteering?

Yes / No

At the center is your opinion.

Draft It

Now use your organizer to draft, or write, your editorial. The writing frame below will help you.

1. Start by circling your opinion from the choices below.

2. Continue your editorial, using reasons from your organizer to explain your view. Also refer to viewpoints from the article.

If you have trouble writing your editorial, ask a partner to take the opposite opinion. Argue your views and write down any new, more convincing ways to express your ideas.

THIS JUST IN

Should Students Volunteer?

I believe that schools (should, should not) require students

to volunteer. The reasons I feel this way are _____

_____

_____

_____

_____

_____

_____

_____

_____

_____

_____ .

✔ CHECKLIST

Evaluate your writing. A score of "5" is excellent. A score of "1" means you need to do more work. Then ask a partner to rate your writing.

1. **Does the editorial make a clear, convincing argument?**

   Me: 1 2 3 4 5
   Partner: 1 2 3 4 5

2. **Is the opinion supported by ideas from the article?**

   Me: 1 2 3 4 5
   Partner: 1 2 3 4 5

3. **Is there at least one word from the Word Bank?**

   Me: 1 2 3 4 5
   Partner: 1 2 3 4 5

4. **Are grammar, usage, and mechanics correct?**

   Me: 1 2 3 4 5
   Partner: 1 2 3 4 5

Check It and Fix It

After you have written your editorial, check your work. Read it as if you have just opened the paper and do not know the issue.

1. Is everything written clearly and correctly? Use the checklist on the right to decide.

2. Trade editorials with a classmate. Is your editorial convincing? Discuss ways to make your points more convincing. Use the comments to make changes.

3. For help with grammar, usage, and mechanics, go to the Handbook on pages 189–226.

Vocabulary Workshop

Add these words to your personal word bank by practicing them.

 **WORD BANK** challenge • development • exploration • valuable

Define It

Complete Venn diagrams to show how words are different and alike. Choose a pair of words from the Word Bank. Write the words on the lines inside the diagram. In the side circles, tell how the two words are different. In between, write how they are similar. Do this for two pairs of words.

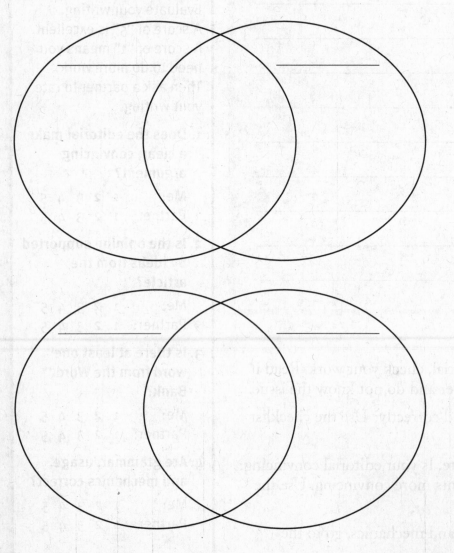

Your Choice

What other new words in the article would you like to remember? List them.

_____

_____

_____

 **Word COACH**

The best way to remember new words is to use them. Use new words in and out of class. Use them when you think, talk, and write.

Show You Know

Write a comic strip in the space below. Use all the Word Bank words in a way that shows you understand their meanings.

It's Academic

Did you notice that the Word Bank words can be used as academic vocabulary? These are words you may use—or hear your teacher use—in your classes. For example, you might hear the word *exploration* used in several different classes.

Social Studies: Lewis and Clark are famous for their **exploration** of the American West.

Science: The first astronauts became heroes for their part in space **exploration**.

English: Our **exploration** of a novel's theme can help us understand the author's purpose.

Math: A trial-and-error **exploration** allows experts to find new math formulas.

Below, write sentences that show ways the academic word *development* can be used in different school subjects.

Social Studies: _____

_____

Science: _____

_____

English: _____

_____

Math: _____

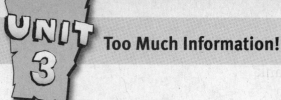

Write About It!

You have read an article explaining information overload. Now you will write about the topic. Read the writing prompt. It gives your writing assignment.

In your response, you should:

- Write an essay about a time you had information overload.

- Include ideas from the article.

- Use at least one word from the Word Bank.

- Use correct grammar, usage, and mechanics.

Writing Prompt

Recall a time when you felt as if you were drowning in information. Write an essay about that experience. Explain what caused it and how you overcame the problem. Use ideas from the article and at least one word from the Word Bank.

accumulate • explanation • factor • reveal

Prewrite It

Once you are sure you understand the prompt, plan what you want to say.

1. Look over notes from the class discussion. On your organizer, jot down ideas that you might use in your essay.

2. Reread the article to look for other ideas you might include in your essay. Add the ideas to your organizer.

3. Look again at your organizer. Are there any other details you want to add? If so, write them in the boxes.

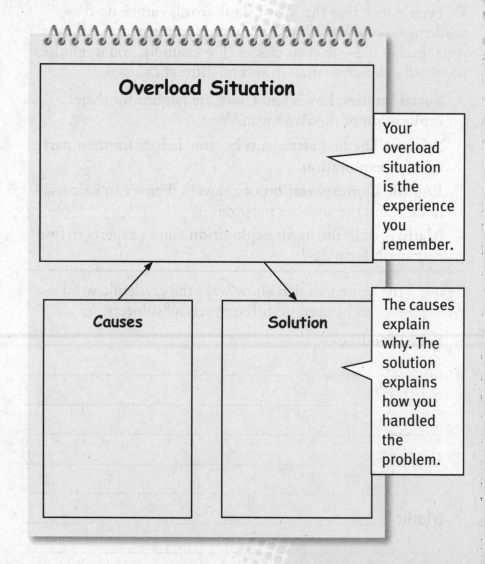

Overload Situation

Your overload situation is the experience you remember.

Causes

Solution

The causes explain why. The solution explains how you handled the problem.

Draft It

Now use your organizer to draft, or write, your essay. The writing frame below will help you.

1. Read the first two sentences of the essay. Use them to get started. Then begin describing your "information overload" experience.

2. Use the notes on your organizer as a guide for your essay. Include information from the article that applies to your situation.

To tell if your essay is well written, see if it holds the reader's interest. Ask your partner which parts are most enjoyable. If he or she loses interest anywhere, rework those parts.

Information Overload

At the time, I could not see it coming. Now I remember it well. There I was, _____

_____

_____

_____

_____

_____

_____

_____

_____

Check It and Fix It

After you have written your essay, check your work. Read it as if you are telling the story for the first time.

1. Is everything written clearly and correctly? Use the checklist on the right to decide.

2. Exchange essays with a partner. Read each other's essays and talk over ways to make your writing clearer. Use your partner's comments to make any changes needed.

3. For help with grammar, usage, and mechanics, go to the Handbook on pages 189–226.

✔ CHECKLIST

Evaluate your writing. A score of "5" is excellent. A score of "1" means you need to do more work. Then ask a partner to rate your writing.

1. **Does the essay explain the situation in detail?**

   Me: 1 2 3 4 5
   Partner: 1 2 3 4 5

2. **Does the essay include ideas from the article?**

   Me: 1 2 3 4 5
   Partner: 1 2 3 4 5

3. **Is there at least one word from the Word Bank?**

   Me: 1 2 3 4 5
   Partner: 1 2 3 4 5

4. **Are grammar, usage, and mechanics correct?**

   Me: 1 2 3 4 5
   Partner: 1 2 3 4 5

Vocabulary Workshop

Add these words to your personal word bank by practicing them.

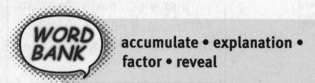

WORD BANK accumulate • explanation • factor • reveal

Define It

Complete the chart below using the Word Bank words. First, tell what the word means. Then, tell what the word does not mean. Use the example as a guide.

Word	What It Is	What It Is Not
accumulate	to gather together little by little	to throw away

Sometimes, it is easier to say what a word *does not* mean than what it *does* mean. If you have trouble writing a word's meaning, first write its opposite.

Show You Know

To show that you understand the Word Bank words, write a clue for each word. Exchange clues with a partner. See whether your partner can identify the correct word for each clue.

1. _____

2. _____

3. _____

4. _____

Combining Forms: *fact*

- The combining form *fact* comes from a Latin word that means "to make, do, or happen." Many words that contain *fact* all have something to do with being done or made, or with something happening.

Factor: Each **factor** Joe named was another reason I opposed the rules.

Factory: Workers in the shoe **factory** produced boots and slippers, too.

Manufacture: Many countries **manufacture** goods that are sold in the United States.

Complete each sentence by underlining the correct word in parentheses.

You may not know that some countries (factor, factory, manufacture) electric cars. Some people in the U.S. would like to see each auto (factor, factory, manufacture) in Detroit make cars that run on electricity. Because one (factor, factory, manufacture) in pollution is car exhaust, electric cars could help us keep the air cleaner.

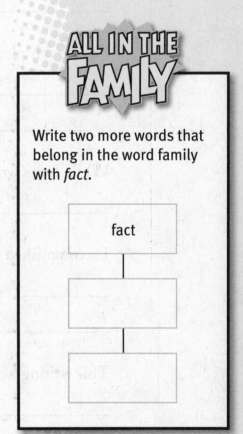

Write two more words that belong in the word family with *fact*.

fact

Writing Reflection

 How much information is enough?

Look through your writing from this unit and choose the best piece.
Reflect on this piece of writing by completing each sentence below.

My best piece of writing from this unit is _____

_____

I chose this piece because _____

_____

_____

While I was writing, one goal I had was _____

_____

I accomplished this goal by _____

_____

_____

This writing helped me think more about the Big Question because

_____

_____

One thing I learned while writing that can help me in the future is

_____

_____

UNIT 4

What is the secret to reaching someone with words?

Rapping About Poetry
Write About It! Memo 104
Vocabulary Workshop 106

Fit to a Tee
Write About It! Letter to the School Board 108
Vocabulary Workshop 110

City Spam
Write About It! Public Service Announcement 112
Vocabulary Workshop 114

Alone in Alaska
Write About It! E-mail 116
Vocabulary Workshop 118

Performing Poets
Write About It! Letter to the Editor 120
Vocabulary Workshop 122

It's a Holiday
Write About It! Guide to a Holiday 124
Vocabulary Workshop 126

My Brother and Sister Drive Me Crazy!
Write About It! Diary Entry 128
Vocabulary Workshop 130

Writing That Heals
Write About It! Flyer 132
Vocabulary Workshop 134

Write About It!

You have read an article about rap as poetry. Now you will write about the topic. Read the writing prompt. It gives your writing assignment.

Writing Prompt

Imagine that your school is holding a poetry-writing contest. Some students think original raps qualify as poetry. Other students disagree. Write a memo to the contest-planning committee telling whether you think rap should be included and why. Use ideas from the article and at least one word from the Word Bank.

connection • cultural • experience • express

Prewrite It

Once you are sure you understand the prompt, plan what you want to say.

1. Review your notes from the class discussion. Remind yourself of points that were made, and decide whether you think rap is poetry.

2. Reread the article. Look for reasons that support your opinion about rap as poetry. Make notes on the organizer on the right.

3. Take another look at all the reasons you have listed. Decide which reasons are important enough to put in your memo.

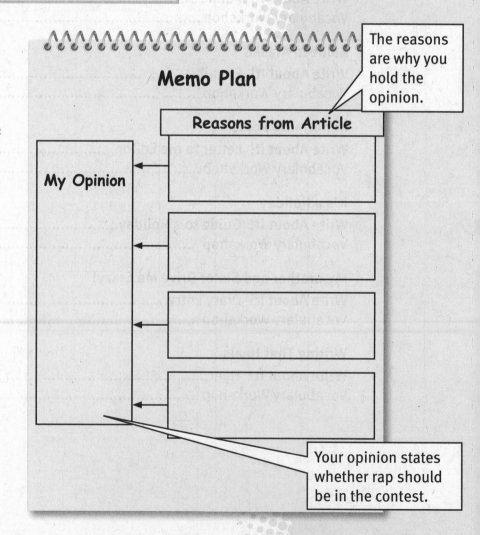

Memo Plan

The reasons are why you hold the opinion.

Reasons from Article

My Opinion

Your opinion states whether rap should be in the contest.

Draft It

Now use your organizer to draft, or write, a memo to the planning committee. The writing frame below will help you.

1. Start by filling in the headings of the memo. Write your name and the date on the lines provided.

2. Read the first sentence of the memo. It states the main idea. You have two choices of opinion. Underline your choice.

3. Then give reasons for your opinion. Make sure you explain your reasons with ideas from the article.

Business memos are usually more formal than e-mails to friends. Do not use the same kinds of casual words you do when writing to a friend. Try to sound businesslike but friendly.

DATE: _____

TO: Contest-Planning Committee

FROM: _____

SUBJECT: Poetry Entries

I think the poetry-writing contest (should, should not) include rap. The reason is _____

_____

_____

_____

_____ .

✔ **CHECKLIST**

Evaluate your writing. A score of "5" is excellent. A score of "1" means you need to do more work. Then ask a partner to rate your writing.

1. **Does the memo clearly state an opinion?**
   Me: 1 2 3 4 5
   Partner: 1 2 3 4 5

2. **Is the opinion supported by reasons from the article?**
   Me: 1 2 3 4 5
   Partner: 1 2 3 4 5

3. **Is there at least one word from the Word Bank?**
   Me: 1 2 3 4 5
   Partner: 1 2 3 4 5

4. **Are grammar, usage, and mechanics correct?**
   Me: 1 2 3 4 5
   Partner: 1 2 3 4 5

Check It and Fix It

After you have written your memo, check your work. Pretend you are seeing the memo for the first time.

1. Is your memo written clearly and correctly? The checklist on the right will help you decide.

2. Trade memos with a classmate. Talk about ways you both might improve your memos. Use the ideas to revise your work.

3. For help with grammar, usage, and mechanics, go to the Handbook on pages 189–226.

Vocabulary Workshop

Add these words to your personal word bank by practicing them.

 **WORD BANK** connection • cultural • experience • express

Your Choice

What other new words in the article would you like to remember? List them.

_____

_____

_____

Define It

Fill in the chart with the Word Bank words. In your own words, tell what each word means. Then circle the number that tells how well you understand each word. Circle "4" if you understand it completely. Circle "1" if you are not sure you understand the word at all. Use the example as a model.

What It Means	connection	
something two things have in common	**How Well I Understand It** 1 2 3 ④	
What It Means		
	How Well I Understand It 1 2 3 4	
What It Means		
	How Well I Understand It 1 2 3 4	
What It Means		
	How Well I Understand It 1 2 3 4	

Show You Know

To show that you understand the Word Bank words, write a clue for each word. Exchange clues with a partner. See whether your partner can identify the correct word for each clue. Use the clue for the word *connection*, below, as a model.

- If two things are similar, they have this.

1. _____

2. _____

3. _____

4. _____

Word Beginnings: *self-*

- As you read the article, did you notice the word *self-expression?* It is in the same family as the word *express.* Break down *self-expression* into its parts to see what it means. *Express* means "put an idea or feeling into words, pictures, or actions." The word part *-ion* means "state of." The word part *self-* means "oneself." Put the parts together, and *self-expression* means "put *your own* ideas or feelings into words, pictures, or actions."

Think about the meaning of *self* to answer the questions.

1. Would **self-educated** people get most of their knowledge from a college or university? Why or why not?

_____

_____

2. Whose address would a **self-addressed** envelope have on it?

_____

_____

3. Do you need to scrub a **self-cleaning** oven? Explain.

_____

_____

The following words are in the same word family. What are some other words that have *express* in them? Add one to the list.

```
┌─────────────────┐
│     express     │
└─────────────────┘
         │
┌─────────────────┐
│    expression   │
└─────────────────┘
         │
┌─────────────────┐
│ self-expression │
└─────────────────┘
         │
┌─────────────────┐
│                 │
└─────────────────┘
```

UNIT 4 — Fit to a Tee

Write About It!

You have read an article about dress codes in school. Now you will write about the topic. Read the writing prompt. It gives your writing assignment.

WRITING RUBRIC

In your response, you should:

- Write a letter telling who should attend dress code meetings.

- Support your ideas with information from the article.

- Use at least one word from the Word Bank.

- Use correct grammar, usage, and mechanics.

Writing Prompt

Imagine that your school district is planning to write a new dress code. Who do you think should have a say in the writing process: Parents? Teachers? Students? Others? Write a letter to the school board explaining who you think should be included and why. Use ideas from the article and at least one word from the Word Bank.

benefit • individuality • inform • meaningful

Prewrite It

Once you are sure you understand the prompt, plan what you want to say.

1. Review your notes from the class discussion.

2. Reread the article. Decide which groups of people you think should be on a committee to write a dress code. Put a check in the box next to their names on the organizer on the right. List reasons in the other column.

3. Take another look at the reasons you have listed. Which are the best? Use them in your letter.

Letter Plan

Who Should Have a Say	Reasons Why
❏ Parents	
❏ Teachers	
❏ Students	
❏ School Board	
❏ Others	

Draft It

Now use your organizer to draft, or write, a letter to the school board. The writing frame below will help you.

1. Read the first sentence. On the blank line, write the names of the groups of people you think should have a say.

2. Read the second sentence. Fill in the blank lines with the reasons why you think these people should be included.

End your letter with the right closing. *Sincerely yours,* is a good way to end a business letter such as a letter to a school board. Sign your name after the closing.

Dear School Board:

   I think _____

should have a say in the new dress code. I think they should

be included because _____

_____

_____

_____

_____

_____

_____

_____ .

Check It and Fix It

After you have written your letter, check your work. Try to read it with a "fresh eye." Imagine you have never before read the letter.

1. Is your letter clear? Have you written it correctly? The checklist on the right will help you decide.

2. Trade letters with a classmate. Read each other's letters and talk about how to improve them. Use the ideas to revise your work.

3. For help with grammar, usage, and mechanics, go to the Handbook on pages 189–226.

✔ **CHECKLIST**

Evaluate your writing. A score of "5" is excellent. A score of "1" means you need to do more work. Then ask a partner to rate your writing.

1. **Does the letter say who should have a voice in the dress code?**

   Me: 1 2 3 4 5
   Partner: 1 2 3 4 5

2. **Are opinions supported by reasons from the article?**

   Me: 1 2 3 4 5
   Partner: 1 2 3 4 5

3. **Is there at least one word from the Word Bank?**

   Me: 1 2 3 4 5
   Partner: 1 2 3 4 5

4. **Are grammar, usage, and mechanics correct?**

   Me: 1 2 3 4 5
   Partner: 1 2 3 4 5

Vocabulary Workshop

Add these words to your personal word bank by practicing them.

WORD BANK benefit • individuality • inform • meaningful

Define It

Complete the chart below using each word from the Word Bank. Give the meaning in your own words. Then write a real-life example and an example that connects to your life. Use the sample answers as a guide.

Word	Real-Life Example	My Connection to the Word
benefit: something good you get out of something	My mom says a benefit she gets from her job is health insurance.	My gym teacher talks about the benefit of exercise.

Word COACH

Ask a parent or teacher to use the new words you are learning. Then use the words yourself. You will remember the words longer if you hear them used and use them.

Show You Know

To show that you understand the Word Bank words, write two sentences. In each sentence, use and highlight two of the words. Use the example as a model.

• A benefit of individuality is that you get to be yourself.

1. _____

_____

2. _____

_____

Partner Up

Trade sentences with a partner. Check each other's work to see if you used the words correctly. Fix any mistakes.

Word Roots: *bene*

• Many English words have roots from other languages. Knowing what common roots mean can help you figure out the meanings of unfamiliar words. For example, the Word Bank word *benefit* has the Latin root *bene,* which means "good." If you did not know what *benefit* means, you might guess it is related to "good."

Use the meaning of *bene* to answer each question.

1. Would you expect a **benevolent** person to be evil? Explain.

_____

_____

2. Would a **benediction** at the end of a program be a blessing or a curse? Why?

_____

_____

3. Would a **benefactor** be someone who helps an organization or hurts it? Explain.

_____

_____

The following words are in the same word family. What are some other words that have *benefit* in them? Add one to the list.

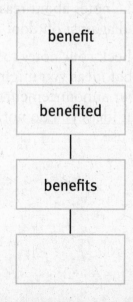

benefit

benefited

benefits

_____

Unit 4 · City Spam

Write About It!

You have read an article about outdoor advertising in the city. Now you will write about the topic. Read the writing prompt. It gives your writing assignment.

Writing Prompt

Write a public service announcement for a radio station. Ask people to go to a town hall meeting to talk about putting limits on city spam. Give reasons why people should care about the issue. Use ideas from the article and at least one word from the Word Bank.

connection • media • relevant • sensory

Prewrite It

Once you are sure you understand the prompt, plan what you want to say.

1. Review your notes from the class discussion.

2. Reread the article. Use the organizer on the right to take notes about reasons for and against outdoor ads.

3. Check your notes to see what ideas you might use in your announcement. Cross out ideas you do not want to use.

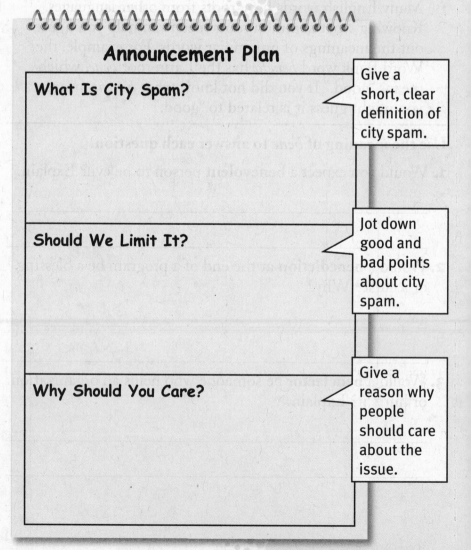

Announcement Plan

What Is City Spam?

Give a short, clear definition of city spam.

Should We Limit It?

Jot down good and bad points about city spam.

Why Should You Care?

Give a reason why people should care about the issue.

Draft It

Now use your organizer to draft, or write, a public service announcement. The writing frame below will help you.

1. Read the first sentence below. It gives the main idea. Then complete the second sentence by defining city spam.

2. Next, underline whether you are for or against city spam, and write a reason why people should care about the issue. Be sure to include ideas from the article.

Writing COACH

When you write a speech or an announcement, your sentences need to be easy to say. Ask a classmate to read your announcement aloud. Is it easy to read? If not, ask for help wording your ideas.

City Spam Town Hall Meeting

Come to city hall this Tuesday at 7 P.M. to discuss limits

on city spam. City spam is _____

_____

_____ .

We (should, should not) consider limiting outdoor

advertising in the city because _____

_____

_____

_____

_____ .

Check It and Fix It

Check your work after you have finished it. Try to imagine the way it would sound on the radio.

1. Is your announcement clear? Have you written your ideas correctly? The checklist on the right will help you decide.

2. Trade announcements with a classmate. Talk about ways to improve your announcements. Revise your work.

3. For help with grammar, usage, and mechanics, go to the Handbook on pages 189–226.

✔ CHECKLIST

Evaluate your writing. A score of "5" is excellent. A score of "1" means you need to do more work. Then ask a partner to rate your writing.

1. **Does the announcement define what city spam is?**

   Me: 1 2 3 4 5
   Partner: 1 2 3 4 5

2. **Does the announcement include ideas from the article?**

   Me: 1 2 3 4 5
   Partner: 1 2 3 4 5

3. **Is there at least one word from the Word Bank?**

   Me: 1 2 3 4 5
   Partner: 1 2 3 4 5

4. **Are grammar, usage, and mechanics correct?**

   Me: 1 2 3 4 5
   Partner: 1 2 3 4 5

Vocabulary Workshop

Add these words to your personal word bank by practicing them.

 **WORD BANK** connection • media • relevant • sensory

Define It

In your own words, write what each word in the Word Bank means. Then think of a word that has the same or a very similar meaning. Write that word as shown in the example below.

What It Means	connection	
something two things have in common		**A Word It Reminds Me Of**
		link _____
What It Means		
		A Word It Reminds Me Of
		_____
What It Means		
		A Word It Reminds Me Of
		_____
What It Means		
		A Word It Reminds Me Of
		_____

Show You Know

In the space below, write a short, short story (just a paragraph!) using the Word Bank words. Be sure your sentences show that you understand the meanings of the words.

Once upon a time, _____

_____

_____

_____

_____

_____

Partner Up

Trade stories with a partner. Check to see that your partner used the words correctly. Talk over anything that needs to be fixed. Then fix it.

Word Roots: *sens*

- The Word Bank word *sensory* contains the Latin root *sens*. This root means "to feel" or "to become aware of." If you remember what this root means, you will have a clue to the meaning of any unfamiliar word that contains it.

Use the meaning of *sens* to define the boldface words.

1. The toy car has a **sensor** so that it does not run into the wall. What is a sensor?

_____

_____

2. My cat is very **sensitive** to sounds and smells. What do you think *sensitive* means?

_____

_____

3. The punch knocked the fighter **senseless**. What do you think *senseless* means?

_____

_____

UNIT 4 Alone in Alaska

Write About It!

You have read an article about Chris McCandless. Now you will write about him. Read the writing prompt. It gives your writing assignment.

WRITING RUBRIC

In your response, you should:

- Write an e-mail about whether McCandless was a hero.

- Use facts and details from the article.

- Use at least one word from the Word Bank.

- Use correct grammar, usage, and mechanics.

Writing Prompt

Imagine that you are the editor of your school newspaper. One of your reporters wants to include a story about Chris McCandless in a series called "Young Heroes." Write an e-mail to the reporter telling whether you think McCandless should be included in the series and why. Use ideas from the article and at least one word from the Word Bank.

feedback • misunderstand • reveal • significance • valid

Prewrite It

Once you are sure you understand the prompt, plan what you want to say.

1. Look at your notes from the class discussion. They will help you decide what you think about McCandless's adventure.

2. Reread the article. Think about the things McCandless did. Make notes about them on the organizer on the right.

3. Take another look at your notes. When you think about all of them, what do you think about McCandless and why?

E-mail to a Reporter

McCandless's Actions	What I Think of Each Action

Draft It

Now use your organizer to draft, or write, an e-mail to the reporter. The writing frame below will help you.

1. Fill in your name and the date in the headings. Then read the first sentence below. Underline whether you think McCandless should be in the series "Young Heroes."

2. Then give your reasons. Use ideas from the article.

If you have trouble figuring out your reasons, ask a classmate for help. Together, turn each action and opinion you listed on your organizers into a reason.

○○○

SUBJECT: Young Heroes Series

FROM: _____

DATE: _____

TO: My Reporter

I think you (should, should not) include Chris

McCandless in the series "Young Heroes."

My reasons for saying this are _____

_____

_____

_____

_____

_____ .

✔ **CHECKLIST**

Evaluate your writing. A score of "5" is excellent. A score of "1" means you need to do more work. Then ask a partner to rate your writing.

1. **Does the e-mail say whether McCandless belongs in the series?**

   Me: 1 2 3 4 5
   Partner: 1 2 3 4 5

2. **Does the e-mail give reasons based on the article?**

   Me: 1 2 3 4 5
   Partner: 1 2 3 4 5

3. **Is there at least one word from the Word Bank?**

   Me: 1 2 3 4 5
   Partner: 1 2 3 4 5

4. **Are grammar, usage, and mechanics correct?**

   Me: 1 2 3 4 5
   Partner: 1 2 3 4 5

Check It and Fix It

After you have written your e-mail, check your work. Imagine that you have never before read the e-mail.

1. Did you write your e-mail clearly and correctly? The checklist on the right will help you decide.

2. Ask a classmate to read your e-mail while you read his or hers. Talk about ways you both might improve your e-mails. Use the ideas to revise your work.

3. For help with grammar, usage, and mechanics, go to the Handbook on pages 189–226.

Vocabulary Workshop

Add these words to your personal word bank by practicing them.

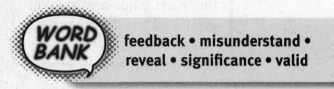

feedback • misunderstand • reveal • significance • valid

Define It

For each set of boxes below, do as follows. Choose two words from the Word Bank and write them in the small boxes. (One word will appear twice.) In the Connection box, describe how the two are connected. Use the examples as a guide.

feedback	**and**	misunderstand

Connection:
Feedback lets you know if you misunderstand someone.

	and	

Connection:

	and	

Connection:

Your Choice

What other new words in the article would you like to remember? List them.

_____

_____

_____

Word COACH

Do not just memorize the definitions of new words. Make sure you can use the words. That way, you will remember them longer.

Show You Know

Write a dialogue, or conversation between people, in the space below. In your conversation, use all the Word Bank words in a way that shows you understand their meanings.

_____ : _____
_____
_____ : _____
_____
_____ : _____
_____
_____ : _____
_____
_____ : _____
_____
_____ : _____
_____

Partner Up

Get together with a classmate, and read your dialogue aloud. Did you use all the words correctly? If not, fix your mistakes.

Compound Words

Compound words are made up of two or more words. When you see an unfamiliar compound, divide it into the words of which it is made. If you know the meanings of the words, you may be able to figure out the meaning of the compound. For example, the Word Bank word *feedback* is a compound whose meaning is based on the words *feed* and *back*. When you respond to someone, you "feed" "back" your response to the person.

Tell what each boldface compound word means.

1. McCandless had a **homemade sleeping bag.**

homemade: _____

sleeping bag: _____

2. He lived **outdoors** in the **backcountry** of Alaska.

outdoors: _____

backcountry: _____

ALL IN THE FAMILY

The following words are in the same word family. What are some other words that have *understand* in them? Add one to the list.

understand
misunderstand

UNIT 4 Performing Poets

Write About It!

You have read an article about poets who perform their work. Now you will write about the topic. Read the writing prompt. It gives your writing assignment.

Writing Prompt

Imagine that a teen magazine is planning to sponsor a poetry slam. Write a letter to the editor explaining whether you think poetry slams are a good idea. Use ideas from the article and at least one word from the Word Bank.

benefit • cultural • meaningful • media

Prewrite It

Once you are sure you understand the prompt, plan what you want to say.

1. Review your notes from the class discussion. Look for good points and bad points about poetry slams.

2. Reread the article. Make notes about good or bad points in the "My Reasons" section of the organizer on the right.

3. Take another look at the ideas you have noted. What is your position on the issue? Jot it down on the organizer.

Letter to the Editor

My Position

Here, tell whether you are for or against slams.

My Reasons

Here, list good points or bad points — whichever support your position.

Draft It

Now use your organizer to draft, or write, a letter to the editor. The writing frame below will help you.

1. Start by stating your opinion. Read the first sentence below. You have two choices. Underline your choice.

2. Then give your reasons. Make sure you explain your reasons with ideas from the article.

The goal of a letter to the editor is to make readers agree with you. Support your position with reasons that matter to other teens. Talk over your reasons with classmates if you are not sure what other teens think.

Dear Editor:

I think it is (good, bad) that your magazine plans to

sponsor a poetry slam. I think this because _____

_____

_____

_____

_____

_____

_____

_____

_____

_____

_____

✔ CHECKLIST

Evaluate your writing.
A score of "5" is excellent.
A score of "1" means you need to do more work.
Then ask a partner to rate your writing.

1. **Is the position on poetry slams clear?**

   Me: 1 2 3 4 5
   Partner: 1 2 3 4 5

2. **Is the position supported by ideas from the article?**

   Me: 1 2 3 4 5
   Partner: 1 2 3 4 5

3. **Is there at least one word from the Word Bank?**

   Me: 1 2 3 4 5
   Partner: 1 2 3 4 5

4. **Are grammar, usage, and mechanics correct?**

   Me: 1 2 3 4 5
   Partner: 1 2 3 4 5

Check It and Fix It

After you have written your letter, check your work. Try to come to it fresh, as though you were reading it for the first time.

1. Is your letter written clearly and correctly? The checklist on the right will help you see.

2. Trade letters with a classmate. Talk about ways you both might improve your letters. Use the ideas to revise your work.

3. For help with grammar, usage, and mechanics, go to the Handbook on pages 189–226.

Vocabulary Workshop

Add these words to your personal word bank by practicing them.

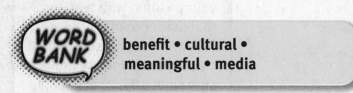

WORD BANK benefit • cultural • meaningful • media

Your Choice

What other new words in the article would you like to remember? List them.

_____

_____

_____

Define It

Complete the chart below using the Word Bank words. First, tell what the word means. Then tell what the word does not mean. Use the example as a guide.

Word	What It Is	What It Is Not
benefit	something good that results from an action	a drawback or disadvantage

Show You Know

Answer the questions below to show you know the meaning of each Word Bank word.

1. What might be a **benefit** of studying hard? Explain.

   _____

   _____

2. Would you expect to find **cultural** differences between people born

   in different countries? Why or why not?

   _____

   _____

3. What song or movie is especially **meaningful** to you and why?

   _____

   _____

4. Would you expect to see the **media** at the Super Bowl or other

   professional sporting event? Explain.

   _____

   _____

Partner Up

Discuss your answers with a partner. Make sure you both understand the meanings of the words. Fix any mistakes.

Context Clues

When you run across an unfamiliar word, use context clues to see whether you can figure out the definition. Clues may be in the same sentence or nearby sentences. For example, the article says, "He brought slam culture to the broadcast **media**." You probably know that television and radio broadcast their programs. Therefore, you have a clue that media might include television and radio.

Underline the context clue or clues for each boldface word.

1. Rima likes radio and TV better than other **media**.

2. Zack saw a **benefit** of practicing the piano: He played better!

UNIT 4

It's a Holiday

WRITING RUBRIC

Write About It!

You have read an article about holidays in the United States. Now you will write about the topic. Read the writing prompt. It gives your writing assignment.

In your response, you should:

- Write a guide to a U.S. holiday.

- Develop your guide with details from the article.

- Use at least one word from the Word Bank.

- Use correct grammar, usage, and mechanics.

Writing Prompt

Imagine that some exchange students from another country are coming to your school. It is your job to help them understand U.S. holidays. Write a guide to one holiday. Use ideas from the article and at least one word from the Word Bank.

inform • relevant • signal • valid

Prewrite It

Once you are sure you understand the prompt, plan what you want to say.

1. Review the notes you made during the class discussion.

2. Reread the article. If there were ideas in your notes that you did not quite understand, clear them up now.

3. Choose a holiday to write about. Make notes for your guide in the organizer on the right.

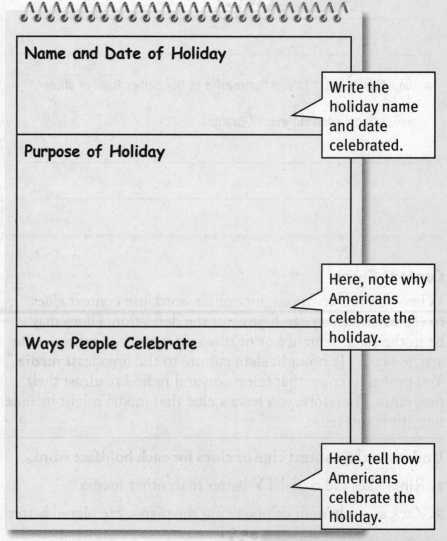

Name and Date of Holiday

Write the holiday name and date celebrated.

Purpose of Holiday

Here, note why Americans celebrate the holiday.

Ways People Celebrate

Here, tell how Americans celebrate the holiday.

Draft It

Now use your organizer to draft, or write, a guide to the holiday. The writing frame below will help you.

1. Start by naming the holiday you have chosen and filling in the date it is celebrated. Then give information about the holiday by answering each question. Use complete sentences.

2. Make sure you answer the questions with information from the article.

A U.S. Holiday: _____ Celebrated on: _____

Why do Americans celebrate this holiday? _____

_____

_____

_____

How do Americans celebrate the holiday? _____

_____

_____

_____

Check It and Fix It

After you have written your guide, check your work. Imagine that you have never before heard of the holiday. Does the guide explain what it is?

1. Is your guide written clearly and correctly? The checklist on the right will help you decide.

2. Trade guides with a classmate. Talk about ways you both might improve your guides. Use the ideas to revise your work.

3. For help with grammar, usage, and mechanics, go to the Handbook on pages 189–226.

People who are new to the United States may not know English well. As you write your guide, think about your readers. Use simple words and clear, complete sentences.

✔ CHECKLIST

Evaluate your writing. A score of "5" is excellent. A score of "1" means you need to do more work. Then ask a partner to rate your writing.

1. Is the guide clear?

Me: 1 2 3 4 5
Partner: 1 2 3 4 5

2. Is there information from the article in the guide?

Me: 1 2 3 4 5
Partner: 1 2 3 4 5

3. Is there at least one word from the Word Bank?

Me: 1 2 3 4 5
Partner: 1 2 3 4 5

4. Are grammar, usage, and mechanics correct?

Me: 1 2 3 4 5
Partner: 1 2 3 4 5

Vocabulary Workshop

Add these words to your personal word bank by practicing them.

inform • relevant •
signal • valid

Define It

For each organizer below, do as follows. Choose two words from the Word Bank and write them on either side of the triangle. (One word will appear twice.) On the blank "because" lines, tell why the two words are connected. Use the example as a guide.

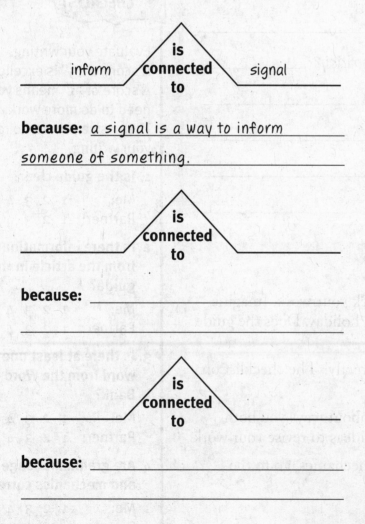

inform **is connected to** signal

because: a signal is a way to inform someone of something.

is connected to

because: _____

_____

is connected to

because: _____

_____

Your Choice

What other new words in the article would you like to remember? List them.

_____

_____

_____

Word COACH

To remember the meanings of new words, try drawing pictures. For example, to remember what the word *signal* means, you might draw a picture of a traffic signal, or light.

Show You Know

To show that you understand the Word Bank words, write a clue for each word. Exchange clues with a partner. See whether your partner can identify the correct word for each clue.

1. _____

_____

2. _____

_____

3. _____

_____

4. _____

_____

Word Endings: -ing

- The suffix -ing is one of the hardest workers in the English language. When you add it to a verb that does not have a helping verb (like *has, have,* or *is*), it changes the verb into a noun. In the article, you read the word *signaling*. The -ing ending turned the verb *signal* into a noun. Look at the difference:

Verb: Helena will **signal** us when the game is about to begin.

Noun: Helena's **signaling** came a little late.

Complete each sentence by underlining the correct word in parentheses.

My family loves (celebrate, celebrating) the Fourth

of July. I cannot (picture, picturing) summer without it.

We (enjoy, enjoying) a picnic in the park. (Enjoy, Enjoying)

good food is part of the holiday.

UNIT 4

My Brother and Sister Drive Me Crazy!

Write About It!

You have read an article about brothers and sisters. Now you will write about the topic. Read the writing prompt. It gives your writing assignment.

Writing Prompt

Write a diary entry telling what you think is good—and, if you want, not so good—about having brothers or sisters. If you are an only child, write an entry explaining whether you would like to have a brother or sister and why. Use ideas from the article and at least one word from the Word Bank.

feedback • individuality • misunderstand • significance

In your response, you should:

- Write a diary entry about having brothers or sisters.
- Use information from the article.
- Use at least one word from the Word Bank.
- Use correct grammar, usage, and mechanics.

Prewrite It

Once you are sure you understand the prompt, plan what you want to say.

1. Review your notes from the class discussion. If something in your notes does not make sense to you, ask a classmate about it.

2. Reread the article. On the organizer on the right, note good and bad points about being a sibling.

3. Take another look at the points you have listed. Use them to decide what to write.

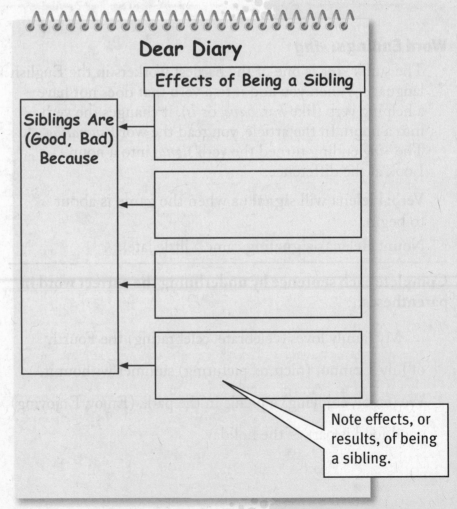

Dear Diary

Effects of Being a Sibling

Siblings Are (Good, Bad) Because

Note effects, or results, of being a sibling.

Draft It

Now use your organizer to draft, or write, a diary entry about having a brother or sister. The writing frame below will help you.

1. Start by telling whether you think it is good, bad, or both good and bad to have brothers or sisters. Underline your choice.

2. Then give positive or negative effects of being a sibling—whichever support your point of view. Make sure you refer to ideas from the article.

Dear Diary,

    I think it is (good, bad, both good and bad) to have

brothers and sisters. (Positive, negative) effects of being

a sibling are _____

_____

_____

_____

_____

_____

_____

_____

Check It and Fix It

After you have written your diary entry, check your work. Imagine that you have never before seen the entry.

1. Is your diary entry written clearly and correctly? The checklist on the right will help you figure that out.

2. Trade entries with a classmate. Talk about ways you both might improve your entries. Use the ideas to revise your work.

3. For help with grammar, usage, and mechanics, go to the Handbook on pages 189–226.

✔ CHECKLIST

Evaluate your writing.
A score of "5" is excellent.
A score of "1" means you need to do more work.
Then ask a partner to rate your writing.

1. **Does the diary entry state an opinion about being a sibling?**

   Me: 1 2 3 4 5
   Partner: 1 2 3 4 5

2. **Is there supporting information from the article?**

   Me: 1 2 3 4 5
   Partner: 1 2 3 4 5

3. **Is there at least one word from the Word Bank?**

   Me: 1 2 3 4 5
   Partner: 1 2 3 4 5

4. **Are grammar, usage, and mechanics correct?**

   Me: 1 2 3 4 5
   Partner: 1 2 3 4 5

Vocabulary Workshop

Add these words to your personal word bank by practicing them.

WORD BANK feedback • individuality • misunderstand • significance

Define It

Complete the chart below using each word from the Word Bank. Give the meaning in your own words. Then write a real-life example and an example that connects to your life. Use the sample answers on the chart as a guide.

Your Choice

What other new words in the article would you like to remember? List them.

_____

_____

_____

Word	Real-Life Example	My Connection to the Word
feedback	When my teacher writes comments on my papers, she calls the comments "feedback."	I am going to use the word "feedback" whenever I trade papers with a classmate and give my opinion.

Show You Know

Write a comic strip in the space below. Use all the Word Bank words in a way that shows you understand their meanings.

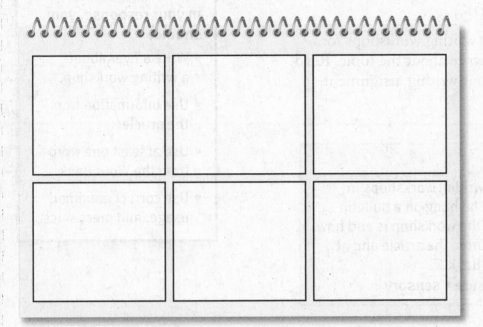

Partner Up

Trade comic strips with a partner. See whether you used all the words correctly. If you did not, fix your mistakes.

Word Roots: *Signum*

- The word *sign* comes from the Latin word *signum*, meaning "mark or symbol." Many other English words come from that same Latin word. For example, the Word Bank word *significance* comes from *signum*.

Tell how the meaning of *signum* helps express the meaning of each of the boldface words. Use the example as a guide.

- I need your **signature** on this paper.

  <u>A signature is a symbol of a particular person.</u>

1. What do you think that statement **signifies?**

2. The city is going to **designate** that area a public park.

3. I use **sign** language to talk with my deaf sister.

The following words are in the same word family. What are some other words that have *individual* in them? Add one to the list.

individual

individuality

Write About It!

You have read an article about writing workshops for troubled teens. Now you will write about the topic. Read the writing prompt. It gives your writing assignment.

In your response, you should:

- Write a flyer about a writing workshop.

- Use information from the article.

- Use at least one word from the Word Bank.

- Use correct grammar, usage, and mechanics.

Writing Prompt

Write a flyer about one of the writing workshops in the article. Imagine that it will be hung on a bulletin board so that kids know what the workshop is and how it might be helpful. Use ideas from the article and at least one word from the Word Bank.

experience • express • measure • sensory

Prewrite It

Once you are sure you understand the prompt, plan what you want to say.

1. Review your notes from the class discussion. Look for ideas you can use to write your flyer.

2. Reread the article. On the organizer on the right, note important details about the writing workshops.

3. Take another look at the points you have listed. Which are the most important? Underline them and use them when you write.

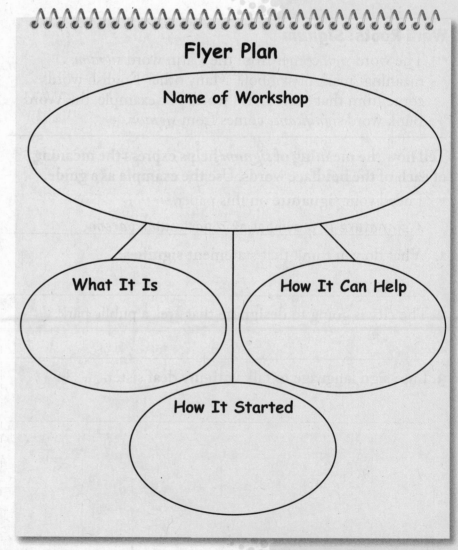

Flyer Plan

Name of Workshop

What It Is

How It Can Help

How It Started

Draft It

Now use your organizer to draft, or write, a flyer about writing workshops for troubled teens. The writing frame below will help you.

1. In each paragraph, finish the thought with ideas from your notes.

2. Make sure you support your own thoughts on this subject with ideas from the article.

Flyers do not have much room. You need to make your sentences short and clear. Write your ideas. Then show them to a partner who can help you get rid of unneeded words.

Could Writing Make Your Life Better?

Consider going to a writing workshop called _____

_____ .

It meets in the school library Saturday mornings from

ten to noon. This workshop is a place where _____

_____

_____

_____ .

Some of the ways this workshop can help you are _____

_____

_____ .

✔ CHECKLIST

Evaluate your writing.
A score of "5" is excellent.
A score of "1" means you need to do more work.
Then ask a partner to rate your writing.

1. **Is the flyer clear and complete?**

   Me: 1 2 3 4 5
   Partner: 1 2 3 4 5

2. **Does it include details from the article?**

   Me: 1 2 3 4 5
   Partner: 1 2 3 4 5

3. **Is there at least one word from the Word Bank?**

   Me: 1 2 3 4 5
   Partner: 1 2 3 4 5

4. **Are grammar, usage, and mechanics correct?**

   Me: 1 2 3 4 5
   Partner: 1 2 3 4 5

Check It and Fix It

After you have written your flyer, check your work. Does the flyer include all the information a person would need to attend the workshop? If not, add information.

1. Is your flyer written clearly and correctly? The checklist on the right will help you decide.

2. Trade flyers with a classmate. Talk about ways you both might improve your flyers. Use the ideas to revise your work.

3. For help with grammar, usage, and mechanics, go to the Handbook on pages 189–226.

Vocabulary Workshop

Add these words to your personal word bank by practicing them.

 **experience • express • measure • sensory**

Your Choice

What other new words in the article would you like to remember? List them.

_____

_____

_____

Define It

Fill in the chart with the Word Bank words. In your own words, tell what each word means. Then circle the number that tells how well you understand each word. Circle "4" if you understand it completely. Circle "1" if you are not sure you understand the word at all.

What It Means	
	How Well I Understand It 1 2 3 4

What It Means	
	How Well I Understand It 1 2 3 4

What It Means	
	How Well I Understand It 1 2 3 4

What It Means	
	How Well I Understand It 1 2 3 4

Show You Know

To show that you understand the Word Bank words, write two sentences. In each sentence, use and highlight two of the words.

1. _____

_____

2. _____

_____

Partner Up

Trade sentences with a partner. Did you use all the words correctly? If not, talk about how to fix the mistakes. Then fix them.

Multiple-Meaning Words

When you use a dictionary to find the meaning of a word, you may find more than one definition for the word. How can you tell which is the right one? Look at how the word is used in the context of a sentence. Then choose the definition that makes sense for that context. For example, definition (a) of *express* makes sense in the sentence below.

I traveled quickly because I took the **express** train.

(a) express *adjective:* traveling fast without stopping

(b) express *verb:* to put an idea or feeling into words, pictures, or actions

Choose the right meaning for the sentence.

1. In this song, there are four beats to a measure.

Which definition of *measure* is right? _____

  (a) measure *verb:* figure out the size of something

  (b) measure *noun:* unit of rhythm in music

2. Does the job candidate have experience?

Which definition of *experience* is right? _____

  (a) experience *noun:* skill gained through practice or work

  (b) experience *noun:* an event you have lived through

Writing Reflection

 What is the secret to reaching someone with words?

Look through your writing from this unit and choose the best piece. Reflect on this piece of writing by completing each sentence below.

My best piece of writing from this unit is _____

_____

I chose this piece because _____

_____

_____

While I was writing, one goal I had was _____

_____

I accomplished this goal by _____

_____

_____

This writing helped me think more about the Big Question because

_____

_____

One thing I learned while writing that can help me in the future is

_____

_____

UNIT 5

Is it our differences or our similarities that matter most?

Mr. Mom and Madam Speaker
Write About It! Paragraph 138
Vocabulary Workshop 140

Work Laws for Teens
Write About It! Letter of Opinion 142
Vocabulary Workshop 144

Holocausts in Rwanda and Darfur
Write About It! Interview 146
Vocabulary Workshop 148

A Meaningful Life
Write About It! Opinion Paragraph 150
Vocabulary Workshop 152

UNIT 5

Mr. Mom and Madam Speaker

Write About It!
You have read an article about gender in the workplace. Now you will write about the topic. Read the writing prompt. It gives your writing assignment.

WRITING RUBRIC

In your response, you should:

- Write a paragraph telling whether gender would affect whom you hire.

- Include reasons from the article.

- Use at least one word from the Word Bank.

- Use correct grammar, usage, and mechanics.

Writing Prompt

You own a gas station that needs a mechanic or a child-care center that needs a teacher—whichever you prefer. An equally qualified man and woman apply for the job. Will gender affect whom you hire? Write a paragraph explaining why or why not. Use ideas from the article and at least one word from the Word Bank.

assumption • common • discriminate • tolerance

Prewrite It
Once you are sure you understand the prompt, plan what you want to say.

1. Review your notes from the class discussion. Jot down your ideas on the organizer on the right.

2. Reread the article. Look for more reasons to help explain your choice. Add those to the organizer.

3. Take another look at your organizer. Which ideas do you want to use in your paragraph? Underline them.

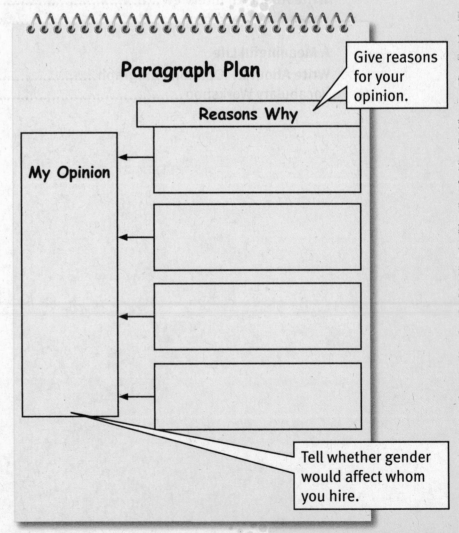

Paragraph Plan

Give reasons for your opinion.

Reasons Why

My Opinion

Tell whether gender would affect whom you hire.

Draft It

Now use your organizer to draft, or write, your paragraph. The writing frame below will help you.

1. Start by underlining your opinion in the title. Then read the first sentence (the topic, or main idea, sentence), and underline your choices.

2. Follow up by giving reasons for your opinion. Be sure to use ideas from the article.

It is OK to use a reason that is not in the article. You can include a reason from your own experience, too.

Gender (Does, Does Not) Matter

If I owned a (gas station, child-care center), gender

(would, would not) affect whom I hire. I say this because

_____

_____

_____

_____

_____

_____

_____

_____

_____.

✓ CHECKLIST

Evaluate your writing. A score of "5" is excellent. A score of "1" means you need to do more work. Then ask a partner to rate your writing.

1. **Does the paragraph clearly state whether gender is important in a hiring decision?**

   Me: 1 2 3 4 5
   Partner: 1 2 3 4 5

2. **Is there a reason based on ideas from the article?**

   Me: 1 2 3 4 5
   Partner: 1 2 3 4 5

3. **Is there at least one word from the Word Bank?**

   Me: 1 2 3 4 5
   Partner: 1 2 3 4 5

4. **Are grammar, usage, and mechanics correct?**

   Me: 1 2 3 4 5
   Partner: 1 2 3 4 5

Check It and Fix It

After you have written your paragraph, check your work. Try to read it as if you have never before seen it.

1. Is everything written clearly and correctly? Use the checklist on the right to see.

2. Trade paragraphs with a classmate. Talk over ways you both might improve your paragraphs. Use the ideas to revise your work.

3. For help with grammar, usage, and mechanics, go to the Handbook on pages 189–226.

Vocabulary Workshop

Add these words to your personal word bank by practicing them.

WORD BANK

assumption • common • discriminate • tolerance

Your Choice

What other new words in the article would you like to remember? List them.

_____

_____

_____

Define It

Complete the chart below using each word from the Word Bank. Give the meaning in your own words. Then write a real-life example and an example that connects to your life. Use the sample answers on the chart as a guide.

Word	Real-Life Example	My Connection to the Word
common : an everyday thing	I have heard people talk about the "common cold."	I think common sense is not all that common.

Show You Know

Answer the questions below to show you know the meaning of each Word Bank word.

1. What **assumption** would you make about tomorrow's weather and why? _____

_____

2. What is a **common** food that teens like to eat, and why do you say so? _____

_____

3. Why is it important that a referee never **discriminate** against a team? _____

_____

4. What is one way to show **tolerance** for other people?

_____

_____

Partner Up

Take turns with a partner reading the questions and answering them. Do the answers show an understanding of the Word Bank words? If not, work with your partner to rewrite them.

Word Endings: -ance, -ence

- When you add -ance or -ence to a word, you make the word into a noun. The endings -ance and -ence are more commonly added to roots than to complete words.

Verb: Ed likes to **depend** on his brother Sam.
Noun: He has formed a **depend<u>ence</u>** on Sam.

Verb: Jan cannot **tolerate** rude people.
Noun: She does not have **toler<u>ance</u>** for rudeness.

Complete each sentence by underlining the correct word in parentheses.

Sometimes, people refuse to (tolerate, tolerance) one another. If people would learn more from others, we might develop more (tolerate, tolerance).

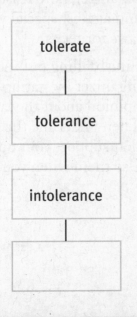

ALL IN THE FAMILY

The following words are in the same word family. What are some other words that have forms of *tolerate* in them? Add one to the list.

tolerate

tolerance

intolerance

Work Laws for Teens

Write About It!

You have read an article about special work laws for teens. Now you will write about the topic. Read the writing prompt. It gives your writing assignment.

Writing Prompt

After reading "Work Laws for Teens," do you think special laws for working teens are necessary? Should they be the same as those for adults? Give your opinion in a letter to your state senator. Use reasons from the article and at least one word from the Word Bank.

class • identify • represent • sympathy

Writing Rubric

In your response, you should:

- Write a letter giving your opinion about work laws for teens.
- Support your opinion with reasons from the article.
- Use at least one word from the Word Bank.
- Use correct grammar, usage, and mechanics.

Prewrite It

Once you are sure you understand the prompt, plan what you want to say.

1. Review your notes from the class discussion. Use the organizer on the right to jot down your thoughts.

2. Reread the article. On your organizer, note reasons for and against special work laws for teens.

3. Finish filling out the organizer by stating your opinion about the laws. Then underline the reasons that support your opinion. Use them when you write.

Letter to a Senator

My Opinion

Here, tell whether you are for or against the laws.

My Reasons

Here, tell why you hold your opinion.

Draft It

Now use your organizer to draft, or write, the letter to your state senator. The writing frame below will help you.

1. Start by stating your opinion. You have two choices. Underline your choice.

2. Then finish the sentence starters by giving two good reasons that support your opinion. End by underlining what you would like your senator to do—change the laws or uphold them?

A good way to end a business letter, such as your letter to the senator, is *Yours truly*. Add this closing to your letter, and sign your name.

Dear Senator:

    As a teenager in your state, I think teen work laws (are, are not) a good idea. The first reason is that _____

_____

_____.

    Another reason is that _____

_____

_____.

    I hope you will keep these in mind and (change, uphold) the laws.

Check It and Fix It

After you have written your letter, check your work. Try to read it as if you are the senator who will receive it.

1. Is everything written clearly and correctly? Use the checklist on the right to see.

2. Trade letters with a classmate. Talk over ways you both might improve your letters. Use the ideas to revise your work.

3. For help with grammar, usage, and mechanics, go to the Handbook on pages 189–226.

✔ CHECKLIST

Evaluate your writing.
A score of "5" is excellent.
A score of "1" means you need to do more work.
Then ask a partner to rate your writing.

1. **Does the letter clearly state an opinion?**

   Me: 1 2 3 4 5
   Partner: 1 2 3 4 5

2. **Do reasons from the article help explain the opinion?**

   Me: 1 2 3 4 5
   Partner: 1 2 3 4 5

3. **Is there at least one word from the Word Bank?**

   Me: 1 2 3 4 5
   Partner: 1 2 3 4 5

4. **Are grammar, usage, and mechanics correct?**

   Me: 1 2 3 4 5
   Partner: 1 2 3 4 5

Vocabulary Workshop

Add these words to your personal word bank by practicing them.

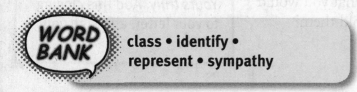

WORD BANK

class • identify • represent • sympathy

Your Choice

What other new words in the article would you like to remember? List them.

_____

_____

_____

Define It

For each set of boxes below, do as follows. Choose two words from the Word Bank and write them in the small boxes. (One word will appear twice.) In the Connection box, describe how the two are connected. Use the examples as a guide.

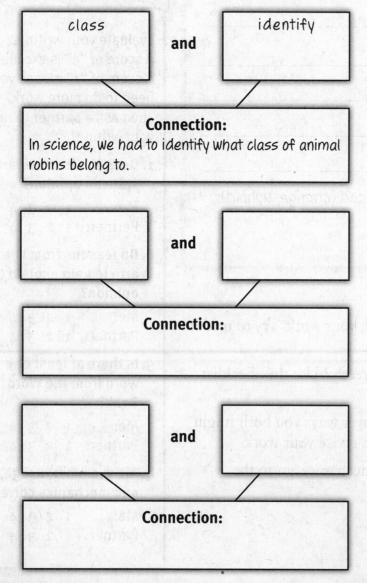

| class | **and** | identify |

Connection:
In science, we had to identify what class of animal robins belong to.

| | **and** | |

Connection:

| | **and** | |

Connection:

Word COACH

When you understand how words are connected, you can use them in more meaningful ways. Using new words together will help you remember them.

Show You Know

In the space below, write a short, short story (just a paragraph!) using the Word Bank words. Be sure your sentences show that you understand the meanings of the words.

Once upon a time, _____

_____

_____

_____

_____

_____

Partner Up

Read your story to a partner. Ask your partner to evaluate it. Were all Word Bank words used? Were they used correctly? Talk over how to fix any mistakes. Then fix them.

Combining Forms: -pathy

- The combining form -*pathy* comes from a Latin word that means "feeling." A prefix added to -*pathy* creates a new word. Here are three common prefixes:

  Sym- means "with," so *sympathy* means "feeling in common."

  A- means "not," so *apathy* means "lack of feelings."

  Tele- means "over a distance," so *telepathy* means "feelings sent from far away."

Complete each sentence by underlining the correct word in parentheses.

When Tom did not make the team, Tom and I seemed to have a kind of (sympathy, apathy, telepathy), because I sensed that something was wrong. I called him, and when he told me what had happened, I expressed my (sympathy, apathy, telepathy). I knew how he felt because I did not get chosen for the volleyball team when I was in sixth grade. I will never have (sympathy, apathy, telepathy) for someone dealing with disappointment.

The following words are in the same word family. What are some other words that have forms of *sympathy* in them? Add one to the list.

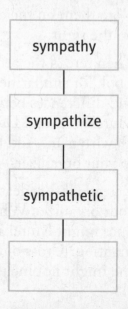

sympathy

sympathize

sympathetic

_____

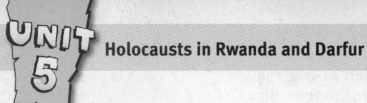

Write About It!

You have read an article about a young woman and her friendship with a Holocaust survivor. Now you will write about the topic. Read the writing prompt. It gives your writing assignment.

Writing Prompt

After reading "Holocausts in Rwanda and Darfur," do you think our differences or our similarities matter most? How would Jacqueline Murekatete answer that question? Write a mock interview with Murekatete in which you give the answer that you think she would give. Use ideas from the article and at least one word from the Word Bank.

distinguish • divide • generalization • judge

Prewrite It

Once you are sure you understand the prompt, plan what you want to say.

1. Review your notes from the class discussion. Do they help answer the question? Note them on the organizer on the right.

2. Then reread the article. Look for similarities and differences between Murekatete and David Gewirtzman. Add them to your organizer.

3. Reread all the ideas on your organizer. Which ones might Murekatete mention? Cross out ideas she might not include.

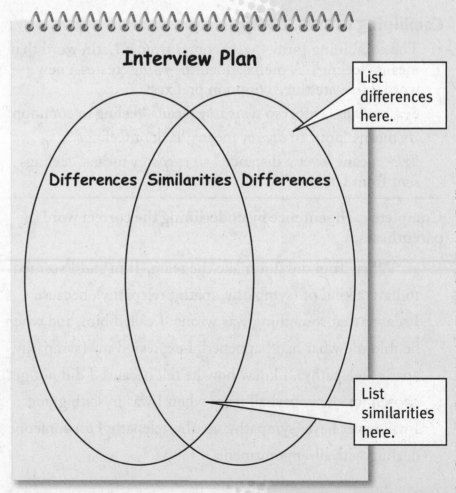

Interview Plan

Differences | Similarities | Differences

List differences here.

List similarities here.

Draft It

Now use your organizer to draft, or write, a mock interview with Jacqueline Murekatete. The writing frame below will help you.

1. Start by reading the question.
2. Then answer the question as if you were Murekatete. What would she say? How can you tell? Include ideas from the article and any others you feel might be true to her views.

Work with a partner if you have trouble figuring out Murekatete's answer. Think about what she did and what she said. What do her actions and statements tell you about her?

Question: Jacqueline, do you think people's differences or their similarities matter most and why?

Murekatete's answer: _____

_____

_____

_____

_____

_____

_____

_____

_____.

Check It and Fix It

After you have written your interview, check your work. Look at it carefully. Make it your best work.

1. Is everything written clearly and correctly? Use the checklist on the right to see.
2. Trade interviews with a classmate. Talk over ways you both might improve your interviews. Use the ideas to revise your writing.
3. For help with grammar, usage, and mechanics, go to the Handbook on pages 189–226.

✔ CHECKLIST

Evaluate your writing.
A score of "5" is excellent.
A score of "1" means you need to do more work.
Then ask a partner to rate your writing.

1. **Does the interview clearly state an answer to the question?**

   Me: 1 2 3 4 5
   Partner: 1 2 3 4 5

2. **Is the answer based on information from the article?**

   Me: 1 2 3 4 5
   Partner: 1 2 3 4 5

3. **Is there at least one word from the Word Bank?**

   Me: 1 2 3 4 5
   Partner: 1 2 3 4 5

4. **Are grammar, usage, and mechanics correct?**

   Me: 1 2 3 4 5
   Partner: 1 2 3 4 5

Vocabulary Workshop

Add these words to your personal word bank by practicing them.

WORD BANK distinguish • divide • generalization • judge

Define It

Complete the chart below using the Word Bank words. First, tell what the word means. Then tell what the word does not mean. Use the example as a guide.

Word	What It Is	What It Is Not
distinguish	to separate similar things based on their differences	to mix or blend similar things

Word COACH

Sometimes, it is easier to remember a new word if you link it with a familiar antonym, or word that is opposite in meaning.

Show You Know

To show that you understand the Word Bank words, write a clue for each word. Exchange clues with a partner. See whether your partner can identify the correct word for each clue. Use the example for the word *distinguish,* below, as a model.

- You do this if you tell the difference between things.

1. _____

   _____

2. _____

   _____

3. _____

   _____

4. _____

Multiple-Meaning Words

When a word has more than one meaning, how can you tell which one is right? Choose the definition that makes sense in the context in which the word appears. For example, the word *distinguish* has two meanings: **(a)** *verb:* to tell the difference between; **(b)** *verb:* to become well known for excellence. Which definition makes sense in the sentence below?

Taylor was able to **distinguish** herself by working hard.

If you said definition (b), you are right!

For each sentence, underline the letter of the right definition.

My best friend is an identical twin, and I find it hard to distinguish **(a or b?)** between her and her sister. My friend is different, however, because she has worked to distinguish **(a or b?)** herself as a fine runner. She has been in the newspaper, and you can sometimes distinguish **(a or b?)** her from her sister by the running clothes she wears.

Write About It!

You have read an article about a Holocaust survivor and the attitudes of suffering people. Now you will write about the topic. Read the writing prompt. It gives your writing assignment.

Writing Prompt

Do you agree that people can choose their attitudes even in the worst of circumstances? Write a paragraph giving and supporting your opinion. Use ideas from the article and at least one word from the Word Bank.
probable • separate • superficial • unify

In your response, you should:

- Write a paragraph explaining whether you think people can choose their attitudes.

- Support your opinion with details from the article.

- Use at least one word from the Word Bank.

- Use correct grammar, usage, and mechanics.

Prewrite It

Once you are sure you understand the prompt, plan what you want to say.

1. Review your notes from the class discussion. Use the organizer on the right to jot down your ideas.

2. Reread the article. Look for more reasons that support or explain your views. Add those to your organizer.

3. Take another look at your opinion. Do you want to change it after rereading the article? If so, make the change. Reread the reasons you have listed. Decide which ones you will use in your paragraph.

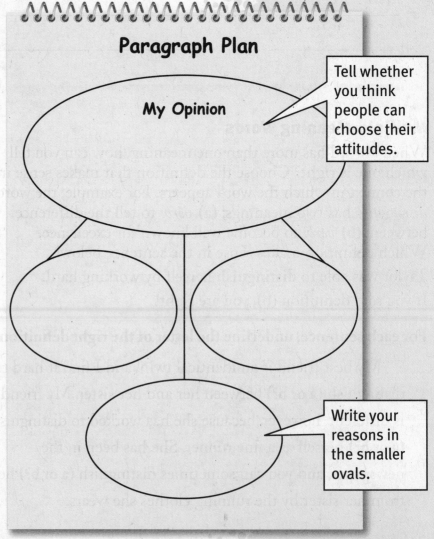

Paragraph Plan

My Opinion

Tell whether you think people can choose their attitudes.

Write your reasons in the smaller ovals.

Draft It

Now use your organizer to draft, or write, your opinion paragraph. The writing frame below will help you.

1. Start by reading the first sentence. Underline the opinion that most closely matches yours.

2. Finish the next sentence by giving your strongest reason for your opinion. Then add more reasons or examples. Make sure you include details from the articles.

Working with a partner can help you find trouble spots in your writing. Read each sentence to your partner. See if he or she understood your point. If not, you will know where to revise your writing to make it clearer.

<u>The Drive to Survive?</u>

I believe that in most difficult situations, people (do, may not, do not) have the ability to choose their attitudes. I believe this because

_____

_____

_____

_____

_____

_____

_____

_____

Check It and Fix It

After you have written your paragraph, check your work. Try to give it a fresh look, as if you have not seen it before.

1. Is everything written clearly and correctly? Use the checklist on the right to see.

2. Trade paragraphs with a classmate. Talk over ways you both might improve your paragraphs. Use the ideas to revise your work.

3. For help with grammar, usage, and mechanics, go to the Handbook on pages 189–226.

✔ **CHECKLIST**

Evaluate your writing. A score of "5" is excellent. A score of "1" means you need to do more work. Then ask a partner to rate your writing.

1. **Does the paragraph clearly state an opinion?**

   Me: 1 2 3 4 5
   Partner: 1 2 3 4 5

2. **Is the opinion supported by reasons and details from the article?**

   Me: 1 2 3 4 5
   Partner: 1 2 3 4 5

3. **Is there at least one word from the Word Bank?**

   Me: 1 2 3 4 5
   Partner: 1 2 3 4 5

4. **Are grammar, usage, and mechanics correct?**

   Me: 1 2 3 4 5
   Partner: 1 2 3 4 5

Vocabulary Workshop

Add these words to your personal word bank by practicing them.

 probable • separate • superficial • unify

Your Choice

What other new words in the article would you like to remember? List them.

_____

_____

_____

Define It

Fill in the chart with the Word Bank words. In your own words, tell what each word means. Then circle the number that tells how well you understand each word. Circle "4" if you understand it completely. Circle "1" if you are not sure you understand the word at all. Use the example as a model.

What It Means	probable
can mostly but not completely count on	**How Well I Understand It** 1 2 ③ 4
What It Means	
	How Well I Understand It 1 2 3 4
What It Means	
	How Well I Understand It 1 2 3 4
What It Means	
	How Well I Understand It 1 2 3 4

Word COACH

If you are not sure what a word means, ask a classmate or a teacher for help. Some online dictionaries are also very helpful. Dictionaries for kids are especially easy to use.

Show You Know

Write a dialogue, or conversation between people, in the space below. In your conversation, use all the Word Bank words in a way that shows you understand their meanings.

_____ : _____
                _____
_____ : _____
                _____
_____ : _____
                _____
_____ : _____
                _____

Partner Up

Read your dialogue aloud to a partner. If the meanings of the Word Bank words are unclear, discuss new ways to make your sentences show the meanings.

Word Beginnings: *super-*

- The prefix *super-* means "over and above" or "more than." The word *superficial* originally meant "above the surface." (The root *facies* means "face.") In time, the word has come to also mean "not thorough or deep in thinking." The prefix *super-* can be added to roots, as in *supervise* (meaning "to oversee"), or to whole words, as in *superhero*.

Use the meaning of super- to answer each question.

1. If you had a **superfluous** amount of money, would you be rich or poor? How can you tell?

_____

_____

2. Would you expect a **supercilious** person to think he or she is better than other people or worse than other people? Why?

_____

_____

3. If someone built a **superstructure,** would you expect the structure to be on top of a building or below it? Explain.

_____

UNIT 5 WRAP UP

Writing Reflection

 Is it our differences or our similarities that matter most?

Look through your writing from this unit and choose the best piece. Reflect on this piece of writing by completing each sentence below.

My best piece of writing from this unit is _____

_____

I chose this piece because _____

_____

_____

While I was writing, one goal I had was _____

_____

I accomplished this goal by _____

_____

_____

This writing helped me think more about the Big Question because

_____

_____

One thing I learned while writing that can help me in the future is

_____

_____

UNIT 6

 Are yesterday's heroes important today?

Heroes Without Haloes
Write About It! Blog Posting 156
Vocabulary Workshop 158

Racing with the Wind
Write About It! Biography 160
Vocabulary Workshop 162

Larger Than Life
Write About It! Letter 164
Vocabulary Workshop 166

Freedom Writers
Write About It! Introduction 168
Vocabulary Workshop 170

The Kindness of Strangers
Write About It! Opinion Paragraph 172
Vocabulary Workshop 174

Honorable Warriors
Write About It! Tribute 176
Vocabulary Workshop 178

Long Road to Justice
Write About It! Debate Speech 180
Vocabulary Workshop 182

Heroes of 9/11
Write About It! Article 184
Vocabulary Workshop 186

UNIT 6

Heroes Without Haloes

Write About It!

You have read an article about sports stars who break rules. Now you will write about the topic. Read the writing prompt. It gives your writing assignment.

Writing Prompt

Write a message you could post on a sports blog. In your message, tell whether you think sports stars who have broken the rules should have their records taken away. Use ideas from the article and at least one word from the Word Bank.

accomplishments • effect • emphasize • occur

Prewrite It

Once you are sure you understand the prompt, plan what you want to say.

1. Review your notes from the class discussion. Pay attention to ideas about punishment for breaking rules. Make notes on the organizer on the right.

2. Reread the article. Look for examples and facts that support your opinion. Add them to the organizer.

3. Take another look at all the notes on your organizer. Decide which to include in your message.

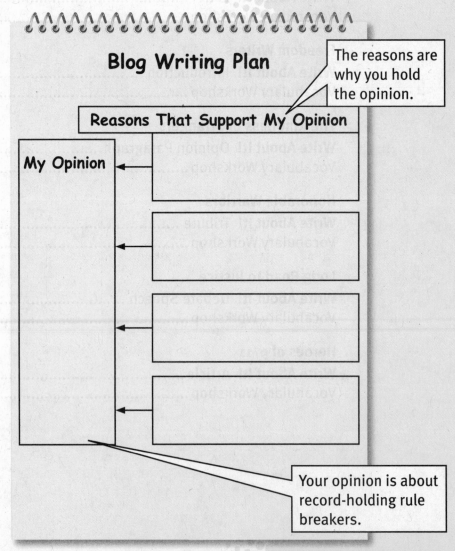

Blog Writing Plan

The reasons are why you hold the opinion.

Reasons That Support My Opinion

My Opinion

Your opinion is about record-holding rule breakers.

Draft It

Now use your organizer to draft, or write, your sports blog message. The writing frame below will help you.

1. Start by reading the first sentence. You have a choice of opinion. Underline your choice.

2. Finish the rest of the sentences with ideas you noted on your organizer. Be sure to include ideas from the article.

○ ○ ○

Record Breakers, Rule Breakers

Players who break the rules (should, should not)

keep their records. One example is _____,

who is in the record books for _____

_____

_____.

He or she broke the rules by _____

_____

_____.

The right punishment is _____

_____

_____.

Check It and Fix It

After you have written your message, check your work.

1. Is your message clear? Have you written it correctly? The checklist on the right will help you decide.

2. Trade messages with a classmate. Talk about how to improve them. Then revise your work.

3. For help with grammar, usage, and mechanics, go to the Handbook on pages 189–226.

✔ CHECKLIST

Evaluate your writing. A score of "5" is excellent. A score of "1" means you need to do more work. Then ask a partner to rate your writing.

1. **Does the message clearly state an opinion?**

   Me: 1 2 3 4 5
   Partner: 1 2 3 4 5

2. **Is the opinion supported by details from the article?**

   Me: 1 2 3 4 5
   Partner: 1 2 3 4 5

3. **Is there at least one word from the Word Bank?**

   Me: 1 2 3 4 5
   Partner: 1 2 3 4 5

4. **Are grammar, usage, and mechanics correct?**

   Me: 1 2 3 4 5
   Partner: 1 2 3 4 5

Vocabulary Workshop

Add these words to your personal word bank by practicing them.

WORD BANK accomplishments • effect • emphasize • occur

Define It

Fill in the chart. In the center oval, write two or three subjects you could write about using the Word Bank words. Use the examples as a model.

Your Choice

What other new words in the article would you like to remember? List them.

_____

_____

_____

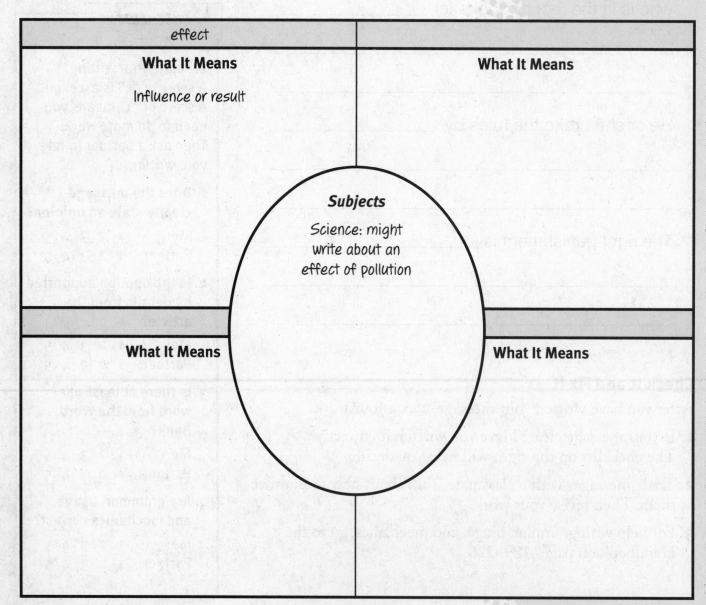

effect

What It Means

Influence or result

What It Means

Subjects

Science: might write about an effect of pollution

What It Means

What It Means

Show You Know

To show that you understand the Word Bank words, write two sentences. In each sentence, use and highlight two of the words. Use the example as a model.

- Accomplishments occur when you work hard.

1. _____

_____

2. _____

_____

Word Sort

Sort the Word Bank words by category, using the boxes below. Read through the article and find more words you can add to each box. Use the examples as models.

Nouns	Verbs
accomplishments	emphasize

Now that you have sorted the words, pick two from the different categories and combine them into a sentence. For a challenge, pick more than two to use in a sentence.

_____

_____

_____

The following words are in the same word family. What are some other words that have *effect* in them? Add two to the list.

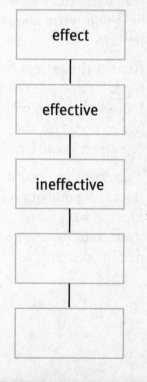

effect

effective

ineffective

UNIT 6

Racing with the Wind

Write About It!

You have read an article about storm chasing. Now you will write about the topic. Read the writing prompt. It gives your writing assignment.

Writing Prompt

Imagine that you have been asked to write an entry about Roger Jensen for a biographical dictionary. Briefly tell his life story, including why he should be remembered. Use ideas from the article and at least one word from the Word Bank.

admirably • influence • outdated • suffering

Prewrite It

Once you are sure you understand the prompt, plan what you want to say.

1. Review your notes from the class discussion. Ask yourself which ideas might help you write about Jensen.

2. Reread the article. Look for facts and ideas about Jensen's life and work. Make notes on the organizer on the right.

3. Take another look at the notes on your organizer. Decide which are important enough to put in your entry.

In your response, you should:

- Write a biographical entry about Roger Jensen.
- Use information from the article.
- Use at least one word from the Word Bank.
- Use correct grammar, usage, and mechanics.

Biography

Note facts about Jensen here.

Year and Place of Birth:

First Big Chase:

Life Achievements:

Year Died:

Draft It

Now use your organizer to draft, or write, a biographical entry about Jensen. The writing frame below will help you.

1. Read the first sentence. Start by filling in the blanks with basic facts about Jensen's life.

2. Then add more facts about Jensen's life. Include only the most important facts. End by summing up his contribution to weather study and telling the year he died.

Sometimes, it helps to talk through what you are going to write. Tell a partner the story of Jensen's life. Then ask what he or she thinks the most important facts are.

Jensen, Roger. Born _____ in _____ .

Roger Jensen grew up _____

_____ .

His first big chase _____

_____

_____

_____ .

His contribution to the study of severe weather was _____

_____

_____

_____ .

Jensen died in _____ .

Check It and Fix It

After you have written your entry, check your work. Imagine you have just looked up the entry about Jensen to find out about him.

1. Is your entry written clearly and correctly? The checklist on the right will help you decide.

2. Trade entries with a classmate. Talk about ways you both might improve your entries. Use the ideas to revise your writing.

3. For help with grammar, usage, and mechanics, go to the Handbook on pages 189–226.

✔ CHECKLIST

Evaluate your writing. A score of "5" is excellent. A score of "1" means you need to do more work. Then ask a partner to rate your writing.

1. **Does the entry clearly sum up Jensen's life?**

   Me: 1 2 3 4 5
   Partner: 1 2 3 4 5

2. **Are there facts from the article, and are they correct?**

   Me: 1 2 3 4 5
   Partner: 1 2 3 4 5

3. **Is there at least one word from the Word Bank?**

   Me: 1 2 3 4 5
   Partner: 1 2 3 4 5

4. **Are grammar, usage, and mechanics correct?**

   Me: 1 2 3 4 5
   Partner: 1 2 3 4 5

Vocabulary Workshop

Add these words to your personal word bank by practicing them.

WORD BANK

admirably • influence • outdated • suffering

Your Choice

What other new words in the article would you like to remember? List them.

_____

_____

_____

Define It

Fill in the chart with the Word Bank words. In your own words, tell what each word means. Then circle the number that tells how well you understand each word. Circle "4" if you understand it completely. Circle "1" if you are not sure you understand the word at all. Use the example as a model.

What It Means	admirably	
do something in a way that people look up to		**How Well I Understand It** 1 2 ③ 4
What It Means		
		How Well I Understand It 1 2 3 4
What It Means		
		How Well I Understand It 1 2 3 4
What It Means		
		How Well I Understand It 1 2 3 4

Show You Know

To show that you understand the Word Bank words, write a clue for each word. Exchange clues with a partner. See whether your partner can identify the correct word for each clue. Use the clue for the word *admirably*, below, as a model.

- If you do something in a way that gets respect, you have done it this way.

1. _____
2. _____
3. _____
4. _____

Word Play

You can make your writing more lively and interesting by using precise words that say exactly what you want to say. A thesaurus can help you find those words. Make your own by filling in the chart below with words that mean the same or about the same as the Word Bank words. Use the examples as models.

Word Bank Word	Similar Words
admirably	really well, wonderfully, perfectly

Rewrite the sentence below. Substitute one of your words for each boldface word.

- My mom says good manners have a good **influence** on people and are never **outdated**.

_____

_____

The following words are in the same word family. What are some other words that have *date* in them? Add one to the list.

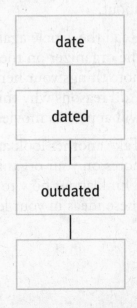

date

dated

outdated

UNIT 6 — Larger Than Life

Write About It!

You have read an article about heroes of the past. Now you will write about the topic. Read the writing prompt. It gives your writing assignment.

Writing Prompt

Write a letter to a movie studio. Present the idea of making a film about one of the heroes described in the article. Explain why this hero would appeal to today's audiences, and suggest an actor to play the lead role. Use ideas from the article and at least one word from the Word Bank.

bravery • effect • exaggerate • overcome

Prewrite It

Once you are sure you understand the prompt, plan what you want to say.

1. Look at your notes from class discussion. See whether they help you choose a hero to write about.

2. Read the article again. On the organizer on the right, note things your hero did. Add reasons why this hero will appeal to moviegoers.

3. Take another look at the notes on your organizer. Think about how to word these ideas in your letter.

Superhero Movie

Hero's Powers	Appeal

Here, list your hero's special abilities.

Here, give reasons why audiences will like this hero.

Draft It

Now use your organizer to draft, or write, a letter to a movie studio. The writing frame below will help you.

1. Read the first sentence. On the line provided, write which hero the movie should be about. Then give reasons.

2. Next, use the lines provided to tell which actor should play the superhero and why. Be sure to use ideas from the article.

If you have trouble getting started, freewrite on a separate sheet of paper about your superhero. Write for five minutes without stopping. Then ask a partner to help you choose which ideas to include.

Dear Superhero Movie Productions:

Please consider making a movie about _____.

This movie would be fun for today's audiences because

_____

_____

_____

_____

_____

A great choice of actor to play the lead would be _____

because _____

_____

_____

CHECKLIST

Evaluate your writing. A score of "5" is excellent. A score of "1" means you need to do more work. Then ask a partner to rate your writing.

1. **Does the letter identify a superhero and an actor?**

   Me: 1 2 3 4 5
   Partner: 1 2 3 4 5

2. **Does the letter include details from the article about why the hero is appealing?**

   Me: 1 2 3 4 5
   Partner: 1 2 3 4 5

3. **Is there at least one word from the Word Bank?**

   Me: 1 2 3 4 5
   Partner: 1 2 3 4 5

4. **Are grammar, usage, and mechanics correct?**

   Me: 1 2 3 4 5
   Partner: 1 2 3 4 5

Check It and Fix It

After you have written your letter, check your work. Imagine that you have never read the letter before.

1. Did you write your letter clearly and correctly? The checklist on the right will help you decide.

2. Trade letters with a classmate. Talk about ways you both might improve your letters. Use the ideas to revise your work.

3. For help with grammar, usage, and mechanics, go to the Handbook on pages 189–226.

Vocabulary Workshop

Add these words to your personal word bank by practicing them.

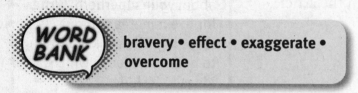

WORD BANK bravery • effect • exaggerate • overcome

Define It

For each set of boxes below, do as follows. Choose two words from the Word Bank and write them in the small boxes. In the Connection box, describe how the two are connected. Use the examples as a guide.

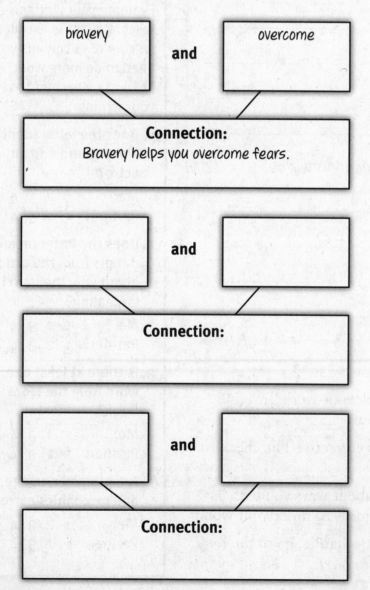

bravery   **and**   overcome

Connection:
Bravery helps you overcome fears.

and

Connection:

and

Connection:

Word COACH

When you are learning a new word, try to link it to a real or imagined picture. For example, you might link *bravery* to a picture of a superhero. The mental picture can help you remember the word.

Show You Know

In the space below, write a short, short story (just a paragraph!) using the Word Bank words. Be sure your sentences show that you understand the meanings of the words.

Once upon a time, _____

_____

_____

_____

_____

Partner Up

Read your story to a partner. Every time you get to a Word Bank word, say "blank." See if your partner can guess what word goes in the blank. Give clues if you need to.

Word Play

- Make your writing clearer and more interesting by using precise words. A thesaurus can help you find those words. Make your own by filling in the chart below with words that mean the same or about the same as the Word Bank words. Check a dictionary or thesaurus if you need to.

Word Bank Word	Words with Similar Meanings

Now try some of the words. Substitute one of your words for each boldface word.

- Ed seems to **exaggerate** his own **bravery** when he tells stories.

_____

Write About It!

You have read an article about young people influenced by a girl named Zlata. Now you will write about the topic. Read the writing prompt. It gives your writing assignment.

In your response, you should:

• Write an introduction to a speech by Zlata.

• Use information from the article.

• Use at least one word from the Word Bank.

• Use correct grammar, usage, and mechanics.

Writing Prompt

Imagine that Zlata, the girl from Sarajevo, is coming to speak at your school. You are asked to introduce her to your class. Write a short introduction that includes ways her writing influenced the Freedom Writers. Use ideas from the article and at least one word from the Word Bank.

aspects • courage • endure • influence

Prewrite It

Once you are sure you understand the prompt, plan what you want to say.

1. Look over your notes from the class discussion. See whether they contain information you could use in your introduction.

2. Reread the article. Use the organizer on the right to take notes about Zlata and her effect on the Freedom Writers.

3. Reread your notes. Which will you include in your introduction? Underline them.

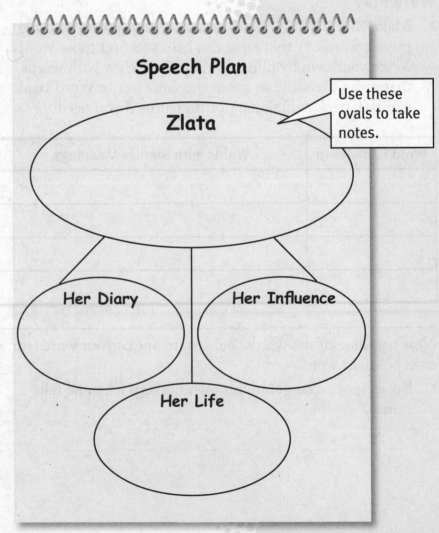

Speech Plan

Zlata

Use these ovals to take notes.

Her Diary

Her Influence

Her Life

Draft It

Now use your organizer to draft, or write, a speech introducing Zlata to your class. The writing frame below will help you.

1. Begin by reading the first sentence. On the lines provided, fill in the name of Zlata's book and briefly describe it.

2. Finish the speech by describing how Zlata inspired the Freedom Writers and how they show—or do not show—the power of storytelling. Use ideas from the article.

If you have trouble putting your ideas in writing, saying them out loud might help. Have a partner take notes, and use the notes to write.

Speech of Introduction

I am pleased to introduce Zlata, who wrote _____

_____,

which is about _____

_____.

Zlata's book helped inspire the Freedom Writers because

_____

_____

_____

_____.

Zlata and the Freedom Writers (do, do not) show the

power of storytelling because _____

_____

_____.

✔ **CHECKLIST**

Evaluate your work. A score of "5" is excellent. A score of "1" means you need to do more work. Then ask a partner to rate your writing.

1. **Does the introduction clearly tell who Zlata is?**

   Me: 1 2 3 4 5
   Partner: 1 2 3 4 5

2. **Does it use details from the article to say how Zlata influenced the Freedom Writers?**

   Me: 1 2 3 4 5
   Partner: 1 2 3 4 5

3. **Is there at least one word from the Word Bank?**

   Me: 1 2 3 4 5
   Partner: 1 2 3 4 5

4. **Are grammar, usage, and mechanics correct?**

   Me: 1 2 3 4 5
   Partner: 1 2 3 4 5

Check It and Fix It

Check your work after you have finished it.

1. Is your introduction clear? Have you written your ideas correctly? The checklist on the right will help you decide.

2. Trade introductory speeches with a classmate. Talk about ways to improve your speeches. Revise your work.

3. For help with grammar, usage, and mechanics, go to the Handbook on pages 189–226.

Vocabulary Workshop

Add these words to your personal word bank by practicing them.

WORD BANK aspects • courage • endure • influence

Your Choice

What other new words in the article would you like to remember? List them.

_____

_____

_____

Define It

In your own words, write what each word in the Word Bank means. Then think of a word that has the same or a very similar meaning. Write that word as shown in the example below.

What It Means	aspects	
steps or sides or parts of something		**A Word It Reminds Me Of** elements
What It Means		
		A Word It Reminds Me Of _____
What It Means		
		A Word It Reminds Me Of _____
What It Means		
		A Word It Reminds Me Of _____

Show You Know

Answer the questions below to show you know the meaning of each Word Bank word.

1. What are some **aspects** of school that you especially like?

   _____

   _____

2. Name a job that takes **courage** to do and explain why.

   _____

   _____

3. Name something you dislike but **endure** and explain why.

   _____

   _____

   _____

4. Who has worked to **influence** you for the better? Explain.

   _____

   _____

Partner Up

Trade sentences with a partner. Check each other's work. Talk over how to fix any mistakes. Then fix them.

Word Roots: *spec*

- The root of the word *aspect* is *spec*. This root means "to see" or "to look." An aspect is a "side" you see when you look at something in a particular way. If you know the meaning of this root, you have a clue to the meaning of any word that contains it. Read the following sentence and, using all the clues, underline the correct meaning from the choices below it.

- The fireworks display at the park was a real **spectacle**.

   a. amazing thing to look at

   b. disappointing failure

UNIT 6 The Kindness of Strangers

Write About It!

You have read an article about people helping strangers after a disaster. Now you will write about the topic. Read the writing prompt. It gives your writing assignment.

In your response, you should:

- Write a paragraph about the effects of disaster on people.
- Support your opinion with ideas from the article.
- Use at least one word from the Word Bank.
- Use correct grammar, usage, and mechanics.

Writing Prompt

After reading "The Kindness of Strangers," do you think a disaster brings out the best or the worst in people? Could it bring out both? In a paragraph, give your opinion and support it with reasons. Use ideas from the article and at least one word from the Word Bank.

accomplishments • endure • effect • exaggerate • overcome

Prewrite It

Once you are sure you understand the prompt, plan what you want to say.

1. Review your notes from the class discussion. Pay attention to ideas about how people act in a disaster. Make notes on the organizer on the right.

2. Reread the article. Look for examples and facts that support your opinion. Note them on your organizer.

3. Take another look at the notes on your organizer. Which ideas are the most important? Use them in your paragraph.

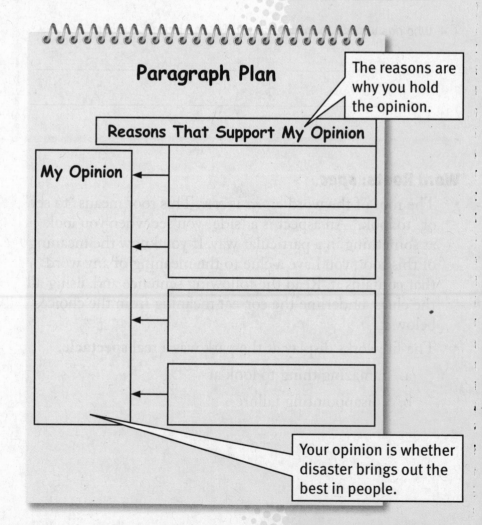

Paragraph Plan

The reasons are why you hold the opinion.

Reasons That Support My Opinion

My Opinion

Your opinion is whether disaster brings out the best in people.

Draft It

Now use your organizer to draft, or write, an opinion paragraph about whether disaster brings out the best in people. The writing frame below will help you.

1. Read the first sentence. You have three choices of opinion. Underline your choice.

2. Then give your reasons. Make sure you include ideas from the article.

To make sure you are ready to write, talk about your opinion with a partner. Your partner can help you decide whether you have a clear idea of what to say before you begin writing.

People and Disasters

I think disasters bring out (the best, the worst, both the best and the worst) in people. I think this because

_____

_____

_____

_____

_____

_____

_____

_____

_____

_____

✔ CHECKLIST

Evaluate your writing. A score of "5" is excellent. A score of "1" means you need to do more work. Then ask a partner to rate your writing.

1. **Does the paragraph state a clear opinion?**

   Me: 1 2 3 4 5
   Partner: 1 2 3 4 5

2. **Is the opinion supported by reasons from the article?**

   Me: 1 2 3 4 5
   Partner: 1 2 3 4 5

3. **Is there at least one word from the Word Bank?**

   Me: 1 2 3 4 5
   Partner: 1 2 3 4 5

4. **Are grammar, usage, and mechanics correct?**

   Me: 1 2 3 4 5
   Partner: 1 2 3 4 5

Check It and Fix It

After you have written your paragraph, check your work. Try to read it with a "fresh eye." Imagine that you have never read the paragraph before.

1. Is your paragraph written clearly and correctly? The checklist on the right will help you decide.

2. Trade paragraphs with a classmate. Talk about ways you both might improve your paragraphs. Use the ideas to revise your work.

3. For help with grammar, usage, and mechanics, go to the Handbook on pages 189–226.

Vocabulary Workshop

Add these words to your personal word bank by practicing them.

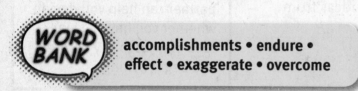

WORD BANK accomplishments • endure • effect • exaggerate • overcome

Your Choice

What other new words in the article would you like to remember? List them.

_____

_____

_____

Define It

Complete the chart below using the Word Bank words. First, tell what the word means. Then tell what the word does not mean. Use the example as a guide.

Word	What It Is	What It Is Not
accomplishments	achievements; goals met through hard work	failures

Show You Know

Write a dialogue, or a conversation between people, in the space below. In your conversation, use all the Word Bank words in a way that shows you understand their meanings.

_____ : _____

_____

_____ : _____

_____

_____ : _____

_____

Partner Up

Get together with a partner. Choose roles and read the dialogue out loud. Then do the same with your partner's dialogue. Fix any mistakes.

Context Clues

When you run across an unfamiliar word, use context clues to see whether you can figure out the definition. Hints may be in the same sentence or nearby sentences. Use context clues to tell what *effect* means in the following sentence:

- The winds had a terrible **effect.** They turned homes into rubble.

Look at the context clue "turned homes into" in the second sentence. It hints that an *effect* is a result.

Underline the context clue or clues for each boldface word.

1. There was no need to **exaggerate** the number of people who helped, because the number was already surprisingly large.

2. The volunteers were able to **overcome** many problems, but a few problems were too hard to beat.

UNIT 6 Honorable Warriors

WRITING RUBRIC

Write About It!

You have read an article about a modern Native American hero. Now you will write about the topic. Read the writing prompt. It gives your writing assignment.

Writing Prompt

Write a tribute to Ira Hayes. In your writing, include what you think people can learn from Hayes's experiences. Use ideas from the article and at least one word from the Word Bank.

courage • imitate • suffering • symbolize

Prewrite It

Once you are sure you understand the prompt, plan what you want to say.

1. Review your notes from the class discussion. Look for the qualities that made Ira Hayes a hero and a lesson we can learn from his life.

2. Reread the article. Answer the questions on the organizer by taking notes.

3. Take another look at the notes on your organizer. Which are most important? Use them in your tribute.

Tribute Plan

Who Was Ira Hayes?

Why Was He Considered a Hero?

What Happened to Hayes?

What Lesson Can We Learn?

Draft It

Now use your organizer to draft, or write, a tribute to Ira Hayes. The writing frame below will help you.

1. Read the first sentence. Use the line provided to describe who Ira Hayes was.

2. Then sum up what we can learn from Hayes's life. Be sure to use details from the article in your tribute.

> A tribute honors, thanks, or pays respect to a person. In a tribute, you can mention the person's weaknesses as well as strengths. However, you try to give a positive picture overall.

Ira Hayes was _____

_____

_____ .

He went to war and was considered to be a hero because

_____

_____

_____ .

We can learn from Hayes's life that _____

_____

_____

_____ .

Check It and Fix It

After you have written your tribute, check your work. Try to come to it fresh, as though you were reading it for the first time.

1. Is your tribute written clearly and correctly? The checklist on the right will help you decide.

2. Trade tributes with a classmate. Talk about ways you both might improve your writing. Use the ideas to revise your work.

3. For help with grammar, usage, and mechanics, go to the Handbook on pages 189–226.

✔ CHECKLIST

Evaluate your writing. A score of "5" is excellent. A score of "1" means you need to do more work. Then ask a partner to rate your writing.

1. **Does the tribute tell who Hayes is and why he is a hero?**

   Me: 1 2 3 4 5
   Partner: 1 2 3 4 5

2. **Does it describe a lesson based on ideas from the article?**

   Me: 1 2 3 4 5
   Partner: 1 2 3 4 5

3. **Is there at least one word from the Word Bank?**

   Me: 1 2 3 4 5
   Partner: 1 2 3 4 5

4. **Are grammar, usage, and mechanics correct?**

   Me: 1 2 3 4 5
   Partner: 1 2 3 4 5

Vocabulary Workshop

Add these words to your personal word bank by practicing them.

WORD BANK courage • imitate • suffering • symbolize

Your Choice

What other new words in the article would you like to remember? List them.

_____

_____

_____

Define It

Complete the chart below using each word from the Word Bank. Give the meaning in your own words. Then write a real-life example and an example that connects to your life. Use the examples as a guide.

Word	Real-Life Example	My Connection to the Word
courage	I heard the word "courage" used on a TV reality show.	I think my brother showed courage when he joined the army.

Show You Know

Write a comic strip in the space below. Use all the Word Bank words in a way that shows you understand their meanings.

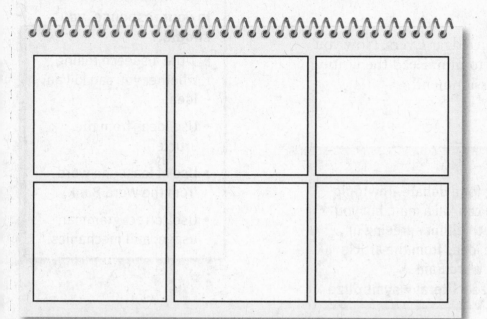

Partner Up

Trade comic strips with a partner. See whether you used all the words correctly. If you did not, fix your mistakes.

Word Endings: *-ize*

- One of the Word Bank words for this lesson is *symbolize*. In this word, the suffix, or word ending, *-ize* changes the noun *symbol* into a verb that means "to act as a symbol for." Another word in the article is *memorialize,* which is a verb made from the noun *memorial. Memorialize* means "to act as a memorial to."

Complete each sentence by underlining the correct word in parentheses.

Many people (idol, idolize) star singers. You probably will not become a music (idol, idolize) by going on a television show. However, it can be helpful to have someone (critic, criticize) your work. A music (critic, criticize) can help you improve your singing.

ALL IN THE FAMILY

The following words are in the same word family. What are some other words that have *symbol* in them? Add one to the list.

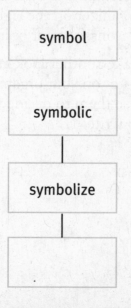

symbol

symbolic

symbolize

UNIT 6
Long Road to Justice

Write About It!

You have read an article about Medgar Evers. Now you will write about a topic related to him. Read the writing prompt. It gives your writing assignment.

Writing Prompt

Imagine that you are preparing for a debate. The topic is a quotation from Evers: "You can kill a man, but you can't kill an idea." Write a speech either agreeing or disagreeing with this idea. Use ideas from the article and at least one word from the Word Bank.

aspects • bravery • emphasize • literal • symbolize

Prewrite It

Once you are sure you understand the prompt, plan what you want to say.

1. Review your notes from the class discussion. If something is not clear, ask a classmate to clear it up for you.

2. Reread the article. On the organizer on the right, note reasons for your opinion.

3. Take another look at the notes on your organizer. Use them to decide what to write.

Opinion

"You can kill a man, but you can't kill an idea."

❑ Agree

❑ Disagree

Here, check whether you agree or disagree.

Reasons Why

_____

_____

_____

_____

_____

_____

_____

_____

_____

Here, tell why you hold the opinion.

Draft It

Now use your organizer to draft, or write, a speech for a debate. The writing frame below will help you.

1. Read the first sentence. State your opinion. You have two choices. Underline your choice.

2. Then give your reasons. Make sure you support your reasons with ideas from the article.

The goal of a debate is to convince people that you are right. In your speech, give reasons that will be convincing to your classmates.

Debate Speech

I (agree, disagree) that "You can kill a man, but you can't

kill an idea." The main reason is that _____

_____

_____

_____ .

Another reason is that _____

_____

_____

_____

_____ .

Check It and Fix It

After you have written your speech, check your work. Imagine that you have before never read it, so that you can look at it with a fresh point of view.

1. Is your speech written clearly and correctly? The checklist on the right will help you figure that out.

2. Trade speeches with a classmate. Talk about ways you both might improve your writing. Use the ideas to revise your work.

3. For help with grammar, usage, and mechanics, go to the Handbook on pages 189–226.

✔ CHECKLIST

Evaluate your writing. A score of "5" is excellent. A score of "1" means you need to do more work. Then ask a partner to rate your writing.

1. **Is the opinion clearly stated?**

   Me: 1 2 3 4 5
   Partner: 1 2 3 4 5

2. **Is it supported by reasons based on the article?**

   Me: 1 2 3 4 5
   Partner: 1 2 3 4 5

3. **Is there at least one word from the Word Bank?**

   Me: 1 2 3 4 5
   Partner: 1 2 3 4 5

4. **Are grammar, usage, and mechanics correct?**

   Me: 1 2 3 4 5
   Partner: 1 2 3 4 5

Vocabulary Workshop

Add these words to your personal word bank by practicing them.

 aspects • bravery • emphasize • literal • symbolize

Your Choice

What other new words in the article would you like to remember? List them.

_____

_____

_____

Define It

Fill in the chart. In the center oval, write two or three subjects you could write about using the Word Bank words.

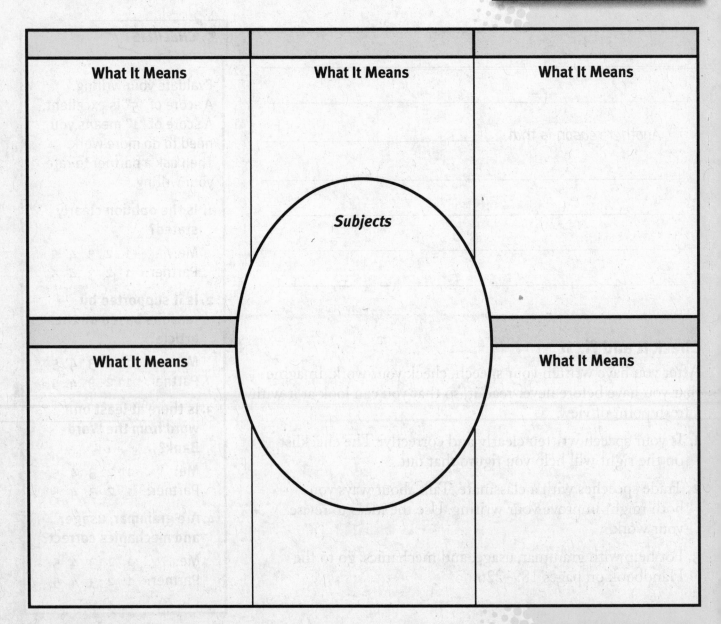

What It Means	What It Means	What It Means

Subjects

What It Means   What It Means

Show You Know

To show that you understand the Word Bank words, write a clue for each word. Exchange clues with a partner. See whether your partner can identify the correct word for each clue.

1. _____

2. _____

3. _____

4. _____

5. _____

Word Parts: *littera*

- The Word Bank word *literal* comes from the Latin word *littera*, meaning "letter." The literal meaning of a word or phrase is the exact, or "letter by letter," meaning. Many other words come from *littera*. They all have to do with words in one way or another.

The boldface words come from *littera*. Tell what each word has to do with letters.

1. Juana likes to read poetry, short stories, and other **literature.**

Link to "letters": _____

2. She volunteers to teach people to read in **literacy** classes.

Link to "letters": _____

Write About It!

You have read an article about real-life heroes of 9/11. Now you will write about it. Read the writing prompt. It gives your writing assignment.

Writing Prompt

Write a short article about 9/11 called "We Remember." Interview at least one classmate for your article. Use ideas from the article and at least one word from the Word Bank.

admirably • imitate • observe • outdated

WRITING RUBRIC

In your response, you should:

- Write a short article about 9/11.
- Include a classmate's memories and details from the article.
- Use at least one word from the Word Bank.
- Use correct grammar, usage, and mechanics.

Prewrite It

Once you are sure you understand the prompt, plan what you want to say.

1. Review your notes from the class discussion. See which notes will help you write.

2. Reread the article. On the organizer on the right, note ideas you can use in your article.

3. Interview a classmate. Take notes on the organizer.

Interview Plan

What Was 9/11?

What Are Your Classmate's Memories?

> Here, take notes during your interview.

What Is a Memory from the Article?

> Here, take notes on a 9/11 story in the article.

Draft It

Now use your organizer to draft, or write, a short article about memories of 9/11. The writing frame below will help you.

1. Read the first sentence. Use the lines provided to tell what happened on 9/11.

2. Read the second sentence. Use the lines provided to sum up a classmate's memories. Then sum up a story from the article about 9/11.

The events of 9/11 were very upsetting. If a classmate does not want to talk about that day, ask someone else to share memories.

On 9/11/2001, _____
_____
_____

Many Americans have memories of that day. My

classmate remembers _____
_____
_____
_____

Other people remember _____
_____
_____
_____

Check It and Fix It

After you have written your article, check your work. Try to look at it with a "fresh eye."

1. Is the article clear and correct? The checklist on the right will help you decide.

2. Trade articles with a classmate. Talk about ways you both might improve your articles. Use the suggestions to revise your work.

3. For help with grammar, usage, and mechanics, go to the Handbook on pages 189–226.

✔ CHECKLIST

Evaluate your work. A score of "5" is excellent. A score of "1" means you need to do more work. Then ask a partner to rate your writing.

1. **Does the article tell what happened on 9/11?**

   Me: 1 2 3 4 5
   Partner: 1 2 3 4 5

2. **Does it include memories as well as ideas from the article?**

   Me: 1 2 3 4 5
   Partner: 1 2 3 4 5

3. **Is there at least one word from the Word Bank?**

   Me: 1 2 3 4 5
   Partner: 1 2 3 4 5

4. **Are grammar, usage, and mechanics correct?**

   Me: 1 2 3 4 5
   Partner: 1 2 3 4 5

Vocabulary Workshop

Add these words to your personal word bank by practicing them.

WORD BANK admirably • imitate • observe • outdated

Define It

For each organizer below, do as follows. Choose two words from the Word Bank and write them on either side of the triangle. On the blank "because" lines, tell why the two words are connected. Use the examples as a guide.

imitate **is connected to** admirably

because: You might want to imitate something that is done admirably.

is connected to

because: _____

_____

is connected to

because: _____

_____

Word COACH

Do not forget to practice new Word Bank words. If you do not use them, you will not remember them.

Show You Know

Write a comic strip in the space below. Use all the Word Bank words in a way that shows you understand their meanings.

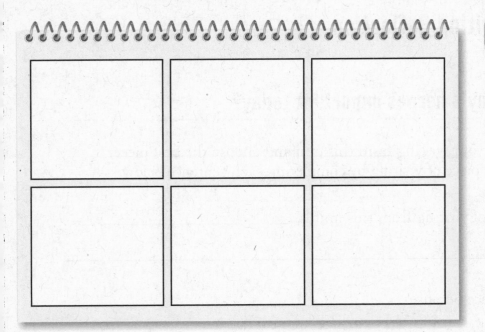

Partner Up

Trade comic strips with a partner. Check each other's comic strips to see if you used all the Word Bank words correctly. If not, fix your mistakes.

Context Clues

Sometimes, you can figure out what an unfamiliar word means by using clues in the words and sentences around the unfamiliar word. What clues tell what *admired* means in the sentence from the article, below?

- "His relatives **admired** what he did and helped pay the phone bill."

   In this sentence, you learned that the way his relatives felt about what he did led them to help him. That tells you they must have thought his actions were good. So *admired* probably means something like "thought it was good."

For each sentence, underline the context clues that help explain what the boldfaced word means.

1. People all over America watched their TVs to **observe** the events of 9/11.

2. In an emergency, no one wants to use old, **outdated** equipment.

3. My little brother does whatever I do, and I wish he would not **imitate** me.

Writing Reflection

 Are yesterday's heroes important today?

Look through your writing from this unit and choose the best piece.
Reflect on this piece of writing by completing each sentence below.

My best piece of writing from this unit is _____
_____

I chose this piece because _____
_____
_____

While I was writing, one goal I had was _____
_____

I accomplished this goal by _____
_____
_____

This writing helped me think more about the Big Question because _____
_____
_____

One thing I learned while writing that can help me in the future is _____
_____
_____

GRAMMAR, USAGE, AND MECHANICS HANDBOOK

Nouns 190

Pronouns 193

Verbs 198

Adjectives 208

Adverbs.. 211

Prepositions.. 213

Conjunctions 214

Sentences..216

Capitalization 219

Punctuation 220

Spelling... 223

Commonly Confused Words.. 224

Nouns

A **noun** names a person, a place, or a thing.

Person: <u>Mona</u> is a <u>student</u>.
Place: My <u>school</u> is <u>Marson Middle School</u>.
Thing: That <u>article</u> is about <u>baseball</u>.

Regular Plurals

A **singular noun** names one person, place, or thing.
A **plural noun** names more than one person, place, or thing.
To form the plural of most nouns, add *-s* to the end of the noun.

Singular	Plural
one teenager	two teenager<u>s</u>
this computer	these computer<u>s</u>
that government	those government<u>s</u>
a site	many site<u>s</u>

A noncount noun, which names something you cannot count, does not have a plural form. Some common noncount nouns are *clothing, equipment, furniture, information, knowledge,* and *water.*

Exercise: Regular Plurals

Highlight and fix the five mistakes in noun plurals.

(1) Roger Jensen was the first of many storm chaser. (2) They like to take photograph of thunderstorms and twisters. (3) Some individuals also enjoy the thrill of chasing hurricane. (4) Several weather station provide information to storm chasers. (5) Most individuals who chase do not get paid. (6) Over the last ten year, the Internet has led to an increased interest in storm chasing.

Nouns continued

Special Noun Plurals

To make some nouns plural, you need to do more than add an *-s* ending. Use the chart to figure out how to spell these plurals.

Singular Noun Ending	Singular	Plural
When a noun ends in *ch, s, sh, x,* or *z*, add *-es*.	a lun<u>ch</u> one dres<u>s</u> that di<u>sh</u> this bo<u>x</u> each walt<u>z</u>	two lunch<u>es</u> many dress<u>es</u> those dish<u>es</u> these box<u>es</u> several waltz<u>es</u>
When a noun ends in a consonant + *y*, change the *y* to *i* and add *-es*.	a count<u>ry</u> one pen<u>ny</u> every ci<u>ty</u>	many count<u>ries</u> several pen<u>nies</u> ten ci<u>ties</u>
When a noun ends in *f* or *fe*, change the *f* to *v* and add *-es*. Note exceptions to this rule.	this lea<u>f</u> one kni<u>fe</u> a chie<u>f</u> one roo<u>f</u>	these lea<u>ves</u> two kni<u>ves</u> several chie<u>fs</u> many roo<u>fs</u>
When a noun ends in a consonant + *o*, add *-es*. Note exceptions to this rule.	that he<u>ro</u> a pota<u>to</u> one pia<u>no</u> an au<u>to</u>	those hero<u>es</u> a dozen potato<u>es</u> many pian<u>os</u> several aut<u>os</u>

Do not use an apostrophe to form the plural of a noun.
Wrong: many belief's   **Right:** many beliefs

Exercise: Special Noun Plurals

Highlight the misspelled noun plural in each sentence. Then fix the spelling mistake. Use the chart or a dictionary for help.

(1) Hurricanes and other natural disasters change the lifes of many people. **(2)** Charitys donate supplies and money to help victims. **(3)** Volunteers have fundraisers, such as car wash's. **(4)** Churchs and other religious organizations may also help those in need. **(5)** They gather boxs of food to send to hungry people. **(6)** Many everyday people become heros.

NOUNS continued

Irregular Plurals

Some plural nouns do not follow the rules. Memorize common **irregular plural nouns** like the ones below.

Singular	Plural
one <u>man</u>	two <u>men</u>
a <u>woman</u>	many <u>women</u>
that <u>child</u>	those <u>children</u>
this <u>person</u>	these <u>people</u>

Exercise: Irregular Plurals

Highlight and fix the four noun plurals mistakes.

(1) Peoples stood near a fence at the nature reserve. (2) Two childs pointed at a squirrel. (3) I asked two womans why. (4) They said the squirrel's fur was white. (5) Some mens said that is rare.

Possessive Nouns

A **possessive noun** shows ownership or relationship.

Ownership: John's coat = a coat that belongs to John

To make the possessive of a singular noun, add an apostrophe and an -s: that boy<u>'s</u> baseball. To make a regular noun plural possessive, add an –s and an apostrophe: the boys<u>'</u> baseball team.

The plurals of irregular nouns do not end in -s. Add an apostrophe and an -s to make them possessive.
Wrong: childrens<u>'</u> shoes   **Right:** children<u>'s</u> shoes

Exercise: Possessive Nouns

Highlight and fix the possessive noun mistake in each sentence.

(1) People disagree about baseball stars home-run record.

(2) Peoples opinions of Barry Bonds vary. (3) Was the teams decision not to renew his contract unfair?

Pronouns

A **pronoun** takes the place of a noun or another pronoun. The word that a pronoun refers to is its **antecedent** (an tuh SEE duhnt).

Jamal plays the guitar. He is also learning the drums.
antecedent   pronoun

Subject and Object Pronouns

Pronouns take different forms depending on how they are used in sentences. A **subject pronoun** tells who or what a sentence is about. An **object pronoun** receives the action in a sentence or comes after a preposition (a word like *for, from, in, on,* or *with*).

Subject Pronoun: She is a very fast swimmer.
Object Pronoun: The swim team gave her an award.
Object Pronoun: Swimming is fun for her.

	Singular Pronouns	Plural Pronouns
Used as Subjects	I you he, she, it	we you they
Used as Objects	me you him, her, it	us you them

Do not use self-ending pronouns as subject or object pronouns.
Wrong: She and <u>myself</u> are on the swim team.
Right: She and <u>I</u> are on the swim team.

Exercise: Subject and Object Pronouns

<u>Underline</u> the right pronoun form in each pair.

(1) Danny Glover is well known for the roles (he, him) has played in movies. **(2)** What many do not know about (he, him) is that he is also an activist. **(3)** Glover produced a documentary following two people as (they, them) struggled to survive after Hurricane Katrina. **(4)** Glover hopes that people will see what happened to (they, them) and want to help.

Pronouns

Pronouns continued

Pronouns in Compounds

Pronouns can be joined together with the word *and*. These are called **compound pronouns**.

Compound: <u>Sam and I</u> went to a movie.
Compound: The movie was exciting to <u>Sam and me.</u>

If you are not sure whether a pronoun in a compound should be in the subject form or the object form, leave out the noun. You may "hear" which form is right.

Example: My dad cooked hamburgers for ~~my brother and~~ (I, <u>me</u>).

Exercise: Pronouns in Compounds

Highlight and fix the pronoun mistake in each sentence.

(1) Javier and me tried out for the volleyball team. **(2)** Him and I practiced serving for many hours. **(3)** Volleyball is the best game to him and I. **(4)** Everyone says that he and me are good players. **(5)** The volleyball coach wants Javier and me to play for the team.

Possessive Pronouns

Possessive pronouns show who owns something. They can be used to describe nouns or in place of possessive nouns.

	Singular	Plural
Describer	<u>my</u> book <u>your</u> book <u>his</u>, <u>her</u>, <u>its</u> book	<u>our</u> books <u>your</u> books <u>their</u> books
Noun Substitute	<u>Mine</u> has my name in it. Did you forget <u>yours</u>? <u>His</u> and <u>hers</u> are missing.	<u>Ours</u> are here. <u>Yours</u> are there. <u>Theirs</u> are missing.

Exercise: Possessive Pronouns

Highlight and fix the pronoun mistake in each sentence.

(1) That volleyball is mines. **(2)** It is not your's. **(3)** The other volleyball is their. **(4)** Hers volleyball is at home. **(5)** Do you want to borrow mine volleyball?

Pronouns continued

Demonstrative Pronouns

The words *this*, *that*, *these*, and *those* are **demonstrative pronouns.**
They point to a specific person, place, or thing. *This* and *these* point to
things near the speaker. *That* and *those* point to things farther away.
This and *that* are singular. *These* and *those* are plural.

Never use *them* as a demonstrative pronoun.
Wrong: Bring me <u>them</u> books.
Right: Bring me <u>those</u> books.

Exercise: Demonstrative Pronouns

<u>Underline</u> the right pronoun to use in each pair.

(1) (This, That) bus stop is far away. **(2)** I would rather wait at (this,

that) bus stop, here. **(3)** Have you ever ridden on one of (them, those)

double-decker buses?

Indefinite Pronouns

Indefinite pronouns refer to people, places, or things that are not
specifically identified. Some indefinite pronouns are always singular.
Others are always plural.

Singular	anybody everybody no one	anyone everyone nothing	anything everything somebody	each neither someone	either nobody something
Plural	both	few	many	several	

Exercise: Indefinite Pronouns

Highlight the indefinite pronoun in each sentence. Write *S* above the
pronoun if it is singular or *P* if it is plural.

(1) Not everyone knows that Tornado Alley is between the Rocky

and Appalachian Mountains. **(2)** Several of us live in areas where

tornadoes have developed. **(3)** Many are nervous when tornado season

starts. **(4)** Most have seen tornadoes before. **(5)** Anybody who has seen

one knows how scary it can be.

Pronouns

Pronouns continued

Pronoun-Antecedent Agreement

A pronouns and its antecedent—the word the pronouns stands for—
must **agree,** or match. To match in number, both a pronoun and its
antecedent must be singular or plural.

Wrong: <u>Nobody</u> raised <u>their</u> hand.
       singular   plural

Right: <u>Nobody</u> raised <u>his or her</u> hand.
      singular   singular

Use the chart to figure out how to make nouns and pronouns agree.

	Singular	Plural
First person	<u>I</u> have <u>my</u> pen.	<u>We</u> have <u>our</u> pens.
Second person	<u>You</u> have <u>your</u> pen.	<u>You</u> have <u>your</u> pens.
Third person	<u>He</u> has <u>his</u> pen. <u>She</u> has <u>her</u> pen. <u>It</u> has <u>its</u> merits.	<u>They</u> have <u>their</u> pens. <u>They</u> have <u>their</u> pens. <u>They</u> have <u>their</u> merits.

WRITER'S ALERT!

To avoid using the phrase *his or her*, make the noun and
the pronoun plural.
Singular: <u>Everybody</u> brought <u>his or her</u> ticket.
Plural: <u>All the students</u> brought <u>their</u> tickets.

Exercise: Pronoun-Antecedent Agreement

Highlight and fix the pronoun mistake in each sentence.

(1) Someone brought their karaoke machine to music class.

(2) Nobody was sure whether they should turn it on. **(3)** Each singer

has worked to master their skills. **(4)** Everyone has their individual

talent. **(5)** The chorus ignored the machine and finished their song.

Pronouns continued

Relative Pronouns

A **relative pronoun** is used to introduce a clause (a group of words containing a subject and its verb). The relative pronoun *relates* the clause to the rest of the sentence.

Relative Clause: Marisa is the student <u>who won the award</u>.

relative
pronoun

Relative Pronouns
who, whom, whose, whoever, whomever, which, what, that

Use relative pronouns to combine two or three short choppy sentences into one smooth sentence.
Choppy: The music is good. The music is on the radio.
Better: The music <u>that is on the radio</u> is good.

Exercise: Relative Pronouns

Use the relative pronoun in parentheses to combine each pair of sentences into one sentence.

1. **(who)** Pete Rose was a baseball player. Pete Rose played for the Cincinnati Reds.

   _____

2. **(which)** Some people said Rose bet on games. Betting on games is against the rules.

   _____

3. **(that)** The commissioner scheduled a hearing. The hearing was intended to uncover the truth.

   _____

4. **(that)** Rose took a lifetime suspension. The lifetime suspension keeps him from being inducted into baseball's Hall of Fame.

   _____

5. **(who)** Rose claimed he was innocent. Rose later admitted his guilt.

   _____

Verbs

A **verb** expresses action or links important parts of a sentence together. Every sentence has at least one verb. The verb is the main word or group of words in the **predicate** (PRE di kuht), which is the part of the sentence that tells about the subject.

Example: <u>Bob</u> <u>is</u> my brother.

The sentence is about Bob, so *Bob* is the subject. The verb *is* links *Bob* to *my brother*, which tells who Bob is. That makes *is* the verb in the predicate.

Example: <u>Bob</u> <u>writes</u> wonderful songs.

The sentence is about Bob, so *Bob* is the subject. The verb *writes* tells what Bob does, so *writes* is the verb in the predicate.

Action Verbs and Linking Verbs

Many **action verbs** name an action you can see—for example, *run, jump, smile*. Other action verbs name an action you cannot see—for example, *think, wonder, hope*. An action verb may stand alone with a subject to state a complete thought, or it may have an **object**—a person, place, or thing that receives the action.

Subject and Action Verb: <u>Darnella</u> <u>dances</u>.
                                    subject   verb

Subject, Action Verb, and Object: <u>Carmelita</u> <u>plays</u> <u>piano</u>.
                                          subject   verb object

Linking verbs do not show action. They connect subjects with complements. Complements help complete the thought that subjects and their linking verbs begin to express. The most common linking verbs are forms of *to be—am, is, are, was, were, being, been*.

Thought Seems Incomplete: <u>Terrell</u> <u>is</u>.

Thought Is Complete: <u>Terrell</u> <u>is</u> a <u>firefighter</u>.

Exercise: Action Verbs and Linking Verbs

Highlight each action verb. <u>Underline</u> each linking verb.

(1) Next week, there is a Sadie Hawkins dance. (2) I invited Jared. (3) Jared and I met in kindergarten. (4) We are best friends. (5) Alyssa also asked Jared to the dance. (6) Jared likes her, too. (7) I overheard their conversation. (8) Jared refused her invitation. (9) He is loyal to me. (10) Quickly, I motioned to him. (11) Her invitation to him was fine with me. (12) He accepted her invitation.

Writing Journal

Verbs continued

Present Tense Verbs

The **tense** of a verb tells the time of an action or a state of being. It may tell when an action happened, happens, or will happen—in the past, the present, or the future. Use the **present tense** to express something that happens or exists in the present, happens regularly, or is always true.

Happens Regularly: I <u>enjoy</u> the sunset nearly every day.
Always True: The sun <u>sets</u> in the west.

Use the chart below to form the present tense of **regular verbs** (verbs that follow regular rules). Notice that the form of a present-tense verb depends on the subject that goes with it. If the subject is *he, she,* or *it,* the verb ends in -*s.* If the subject is *I, you, we,* or *they,* the verb does not end in -*s.*

Singular	Plural
I <u>like</u> you <u>like</u> he, she, it <u>likes</u>	we <u>like</u> you <u>like</u> they <u>like</u>

If a subject is a noun and you are not sure which verb form to use, change the noun into the pronoun that could substitute for it. Then use the chart.

Noun Subject: <u>Victor</u> (like, likes) rap.
Pronoun Subject: *Victor = he.* <u>Victor</u> (like, <u>likes</u>) rap.

Exercise: Present Tense Verbs

<u>Underline</u> the right verb form in parentheses. Use the chart if you need to.

(1) A school dress code (guide, guides) students' decisions about clothing. **(2)** Some students (like, likes) dress codes. **(3)** Some parents also (support, supports) dress codes. **(4)** Other students (disagree, disagrees). **(5)** I (think, thinks) dress codes are a good thing. **(6)** They (make, makes) students safer. **(7)** You (agree, agrees), don't you?

Verbs continued

Tricky Present Tense Verbs

Some verbs do not form the present tense in the regular way, by adding -s. The only way to learn tricky verbs like *have*, *do*, and *be* is to memorize them. Study the chart.

	To Have	To Do	To Be
Singular	I <u>have</u> (<u>haven't</u>) you <u>have</u> (<u>haven't</u>) he, she, it <u>has</u> (<u>hasn't</u>)	I <u>do</u> (<u>don't</u>) you <u>do</u> (<u>don't</u>) he, she, it <u>does</u> (<u>doesn't</u>)	I am (<u>I'm</u> not) you are (<u>aren't</u>) he, she, it <u>is</u>, (<u>isn't</u>)
Plural	we <u>have</u> (<u>haven't</u>) you <u>have</u> (<u>haven't</u>) they <u>have</u> (<u>haven't</u>)	we <u>do</u> (<u>don't</u>) you <u>do</u> (<u>don't</u>) they <u>do</u> (<u>don't</u>)	we <u>are</u> (<u>aren't</u>) you <u>are</u> (<u>aren't</u>) they <u>are</u> (<u>aren't</u>)

These tricky verbs can stand alone as **main verbs,** or they can be helping verbs. A **helping verb** helps a main verb express when an action happened or a situation existed.

Main Verb: Sinclair <u>has</u> a cell phone.
Helping Verb + Main Verb: Sinclair <u>has</u> <u>called</u> me on her phone.

 Avoid using *ain't.*
Wrong: I <u>ain't</u> tired.
Right: I <u>am</u> <u>not</u> tired. OR <u>I'm</u> <u>not</u> tired.

Exercise: Tricky Present Tense Verbs

Highlight and fix the six verb mistakes in the paragraph.

(1) I am sick today. **(2)** It don't seem fair. **(3)** I have been excited about the talent show for months. **(4)** My friends hasn't heard me play. **(5)** I ain't been playing guitar very long. **(6)** It have been only a few months. **(7)** I has my own guitar. **(8)** It is brand new. **(9)** Guitars is expensive. **(10)** I don't want to miss the show!

Verbs continued

Agreement with Compound Subjects

A **compound subject** is two or more subjects joined by the word *and* or *or*. When the subjects are joined by *and*, the compound subject is usually plural. To match, or agree, with this compound subject, the verb must be in the plural form. When subjects are joined by *or*, the verb agrees with the subject closer to it, whether singular or plural.

Compound with *And:* <u>Benoit and I</u> (is, <u>are</u>) friends.
Compound with *Or:* Benoit or <u>I</u> (<u>am</u>, is, are) happy to help.
Compound with *Or:* I or <u>Benoit</u> (am, <u>is</u>, are) happy to help.

Exercise: Agreement with Compound Subjects

Highlight and fix the three verb mistakes.

(1) Candi and Billie are actors. **(2)** Billie and I is best friends.

(3) Candi or Billie have been chosen for the lead in the school play.

(4) The director or his assistant know which girl has been chosen.

(5) You and I have to wait to find out.

Agreement in Questions

In most questions, all or part of the verb comes before the subject. The verb at the beginning of a question must agree with the subject.

Statement: <u>Thomasina</u> <u>is</u> <u>going</u> to the party.
              subject   verb

Question: <u>Is</u> <u>Thomasina</u> <u>going</u> to the party?
          verb   subject   verb

Exercise: Agreement in Questions

For each sentence, <u>underline</u> the right verb in parentheses.

(1) (Do, Does) you know about the civil rights movement?

(2) What (do, does) you know about Megar Evers's life? **(3)** (Have, Has) you read the biography of him in our social studies book?

(4) (Weren't, Wasn't) he a civil rights leader? **(5)** (Are, Is) a school named in his honor?

Verbs continued

Past and Perfect Tenses

Use the **past tense** of a verb to show that something has already happened. To form the past tense of a regular verb, add an *-ed* ending.

Past: Yesterday, Lucie <u>called</u> me on her new phone.

Use the **present perfect tense** to express action that happened in the past or a situation that existed at a certain time in the past. To form the present perfect, use the helping verb *has* or *have*.

Present Perfect: People <u>have</u> <u>used</u> cell phones since the 1970s.

Use the **past perfect tense** to express an action that was completed before another action in the past. To form the past perfect, use the helping verb *had*.

Past Perfect: I <u>had</u> already <u>left</u> the house when Lucie called.

	Present Perfect *have* or *has* + verb + *-ed*	**Past Perfect** *had* + verb + *-ed*
Singular	I <u>have</u> <u>walked</u> you <u>have</u> <u>walked</u> he, she, it <u>has</u> <u>walked</u>	I <u>had</u> <u>walked</u> you <u>had</u> <u>walked</u> he, she, it <u>had</u> <u>walked</u>
Plural	we <u>have</u> <u>walked</u> you <u>have</u> <u>walked</u> they <u>have</u> <u>walked</u>	we <u>had</u> <u>walked</u> you <u>had</u> <u>walked</u> they <u>had</u> <u>walked</u>

WRITER'S ALERT!

Remember to make the helping verb agree in number with the subject.

Wrong: <u>Haven't</u> <u>he</u> listened to the news?

Right: <u>Hasn't</u> <u>he</u> listened to the news?

Exercise: Past and Perfect Tenses

Highlight and fix the verb mistake in each sentence.

(1) Matt has live in Florida all his life. **(2)** By the time he was two, he had learn to swim. **(3)** For many years, he has work as a lifeguard at a pool. **(4)** Last week, Matt apply to lifeguard at the beach.

(5) He haven't received a call about the job yet.

Verbs continued

Irregular Verbs 1: Past and Perfect of *To Be*

Irregular verbs do not take an *-ed* ending to form the past and perfect tenses. The most irregular verb in English is *to be*.

	Past Tense	Present Perfect Tense
Singular	I <u>was</u> (<u>wasn't</u>) you <u>were</u> (<u>weren't</u>) he, she it <u>was</u> (<u>wasn't</u>)	I <u>have</u> (<u>haven't</u>) <u>been</u> you <u>have</u> (<u>haven't</u>) <u>been</u> he, she, it <u>has</u> (<u>hasn't</u>) <u>been</u>
Plural	we <u>were</u> (<u>weren't</u>) you <u>were</u> (<u>weren't</u>) they <u>were</u> (<u>weren't</u>)	we <u>have</u> (<u>haven't</u>) <u>been</u> you <u>have</u> (<u>haven't</u>) <u>been</u> they <u>have</u> (<u>haven't</u>) <u>been</u>

	Past Perfect Tense
Singular	I <u>had</u> (<u>hadn't</u>) <u>been</u> you <u>had</u> (<u>hadn't</u>) <u>been</u> he, she, it <u>had</u> (<u>hadn't</u>) <u>been</u>
Plural	we <u>had</u> (<u>hadn't</u>) <u>been</u> you <u>had</u> (<u>hadn't</u>) <u>been</u> they <u>had</u> (<u>hadn't</u>) <u>been</u>

Exercise: Irregular Verbs 1: Past and Perfect of *To Be*

Highlight and fix the four verb mistakes.

(1) I was excited. **(2)** My favorite cousins was here! **(3)** They hadn't been here for a long time. **(4)** In no time at all, we was at the park. **(5)** My cousin Will was ready for baseball. **(6)** He have been a Little League pitcher for years. **(7)** Once again, his pitches were too fast for me. **(8)** They was faster than ever!

Irregular Verbs 2: Past and Perfect That Stay the Same

Some irregular verbs keep the same form for every tense. The most common are *cost, cut, hit, let, put, read, set,* and *shut.*

Present: I <u>read</u> every day.
Past: Yesterday, I <u>read</u> the sports pages.
Present Perfect: I <u>have</u> <u>read</u> ten books this year.
Past Perfect: My mom gave me a book, but I <u>had</u> already <u>read</u> it.

Verbs continued

Irregular Verbs 3: Past and Perfect That Change Vowels

Some irregular verbs change only a vowel to go from present tense to past or perfect. Others add -n or -en to form the perfect tenses.

Present Tense	Past Tense	Perfect Tenses (has, have, had)
become	became	become
begin	began	begun
break	broke	broken
come	came	come
drink	drank	drunk
drive	drove	driven
forget	forgot	forgotten
give	gave	given
grow	grew	grown
know	knew	known
ride	rode	ridden
ring	rang	rung
rise	rose	risen
run	ran	run
see	saw	seen
sing	sang	sung
sit	sat	sat
speak	spoke	spoken
swim	swam	swum
write	wrote	written

Exercise: Irregular Verbs 3: Past and Perfect That Change Vowels

Highlight and fix the verb mistake in each sentence.

(1) The last time I speaked to Amber, she promised to visit during spring break. (2) She moved in January, and I have not saw her since. (3) Had she broke her promise? (4) Then the phone rung. (5) I knowed it was Amber. (6) She had not forgot after all.

Verbs continued

Irregular Verbs 4: Past and Perfect That Change Completely

Some verbs change their form completely to form the past or perfect tenses. Many of them (like *bring* and *buy*) have the same form for both past and perfect tenses. A few (like *do* and *fly*) change to different forms for past and perfect tenses.

Present Tense	Past Tense	Perfect Tenses (has, have, had)
bring	brought	brought
buy	bought	bought
catch	caught	caught
do	did	done
fight	fought	fought
find	found	found
fly	flew	flown
go	went	gone
sell	sold	sold
take	took	taken
teach	taught	taught
think	thought	thought

Exercise: Irregular Verbs 4: Past and Perfect That Change Completely

Highlight and fix the verb mistake in each sentence.

(1) My family just boughten a new house. (2) We had went to see a lot of houses before we found it. (3) At one house, jets flyed low overhead. (4) The real estate agent had brang us to a noisy neighborhood. (5) My parents thunk it was too noisy. (6) Then we find the perfect home for our family. (7) The house selled for a low price. (8) My parents done well.

Verbs continued

Verbs as Describers

Certain verb forms can act as describers. These **verbals** describe nouns or pronouns. Verbals can end in *-ing, -ed,* or, when the verb is irregular, the perfect form. Be sure to use the right ending or form.

Verbal with *-ing* ending: A <u>freezing</u> rain fell.

Verbal with *-ed* ending: Chantel wore <u>faded</u> jeans.

Verbal in Perfect Form: Her jacket has a <u>broken</u> zipper.

Exercise: Verbs as Describers

Highlight and fix the three mistakes in verbals.

(1) At my house, Saturday is cooking day. **(2)** My mom always makes fry chicken. **(3)** She also makes mash potatoes and chopped salad. **(4)** For dessert, we have froze yogurt or a freshly baked pie.

Future Tense

The **future tense** expresses that action will happen in the future. To form the future tense, use the helping verb *will* and a main verb.

Present: I <u>walk</u> to school every day.
Future: I <u>will</u> <u>walk</u> to soccer practice after school today.

Exercise: Future Tense

Change each underlined verb to future tense.

(1) We _____ <u>go</u> on a field trip to the Carnegie Museum.

(2) We _____ <u>visit</u> an art exhibition. **(3)** We _____ <u>eat</u> lunch in the museum cafeteria. **(4)** We _____ <u>return</u> to school at the end of the day. **(5)** Then we _____ <u>discuss</u> our field trip.

Verbs continued

Progressive Tenses

The **progressive tense** expresses action in progress, or still happening. To form present and past progressive, use a form of *to be* and a main verb with an *-ing* ending. To form the future progressive, add the future-tense helping word *will*.

Present Progressive: I <u>am</u> <u>biking</u>.
Past Progressive: I <u>was</u> <u>biking</u>.
Future Progressive: I <u>will be</u> <u>biking</u>.

Exercise: Progressive Tenses

Write a sentence to answer each question below. Make sure your answers are in the correct tenses.

1. What are you studying in English class?

_____

2. What were you doing early this morning?

_____

3. What will you be doing this weekend?

_____

Modals

Modals are helping verbs. They include *can, could, will, would, must, should, may, might,* and *ought to*. A main verb paired with a modal never takes a verb ending such as *-ed* or *-s*. It does not change form.

Wrong: I <u>should</u> **called** him.   **Right:** I <u>should</u> **call** him.
Wrong: She <u>can</u> **sings**.   **Right:** She <u>can</u> **sing**.

Exercise: Modals

Highlight and fix the verb mistake in each sentence.

(1) You should participated in school activities. (2) I would joining the drama club even if my friends were not in it. (3) Yvonne might plays soccer in the fall. (4) She would played goalie if she had not been injured. (5) I cannot takes her place. (6) I might tried out for a different position on the soccer team.

Adjectives

Adjectives describe nouns and pronouns. Adjectives answer these questions: *Which one? What kind? How many? How much?*

Which One: The <u>blue</u> coat is mine.

What Kind: It is a <u>wool</u> coat.

How Many: I own <u>two</u> coats.

How Much: That is <u>enough</u> coats for anyone.

Articles

The most often used adjectives are the **articles** *a*, *an*, and *the*. *The* is called a **definite article,** because it is used to refer to a particular person, place, or thing. *A* and *an* are called **indefinite articles,** because they do not refer to a particular person, place, or thing.

Definite Article: Buy your ticket from <u>the</u> man in the booth.

Indefinite Article: <u>A</u> ticket costs $10.

Use *a* with words that begin with a consonant sound. Use *an* with words that begin with a vowel sound. (It is the *sound* that matters, not the spelling.)

A: <u>a</u> <u>c</u>ar, <u>a</u> <u>s</u>ong, <u>a</u> <u>u</u>nit (*u* with the consonant *y* sound)
An: <u>an</u> <u>a</u>nt, <u>an</u> <u>o</u>live, <u>an</u> <u>u</u>mbrella (*u* with the vowel *u* sound)

Use *a* or *an* if the noun can be counted. Use *the* if the noun cannot be counted.

Countable: I spilled a <u>cup</u> of coffee. (You can count cups.)

Uncountable: I spilled <u>the</u> <u>coffee</u>. (You cannot count coffee that is not in a cup.)

Exercise: Articles

Highlight and fix the three mistakes involving articles.

(1) Every year, my school holds an art contest. **(2)** The judges are from an union of professional artists. **(3)** Any student can enter the drawing, photograph, or painting in the contest. **(4)** The judges decide which is the best art work in each category. **(5)** I made an original work of art. **(6)** I mixed paint with a rain water from a puddle.

Adjectives continued

Adjectives That Compare

Adjectives can be used to make comparisons. Use the **comparative** (kuhm PER uh tiv) **adjective** form to compare two people, places, or things. To form the comparative of one-syllable adjectives and many two-syllable adjectives, add *-er*. To form the comparative of adjectives of three or more syllables, add *more* or *less* before the adjective.

One-Syllable Adjective: Sara is <u>younger</u> than I am.
Three-Syllable Adjective: I am <u>more</u> <u>athletic</u> than she is.

 Some adjectives can take a comparative or a superlative ending OR *more* or *most*. When in doubt, check a dictionary.

Use the **superlative** (soo PUHR luh tiv) **adjective** form to compare three or more people, places, or things. To form the superlative of one-syllable adjectives and many two-syllable adjectives, add *-est*. To form the superlative of adjectives of three or more syllables, add the word *most* or *least* in front of the adjective.

One-Syllable Adjective: Caryn is the <u>oldest</u> girl in our family.
Three-Syllable Adjective: She is our <u>most</u> <u>talented</u> musician.

 Some adjectives can take a comparative or superlative ending OR *more* or *most*. When in doubt, check a dictionary.

Exercise: Adjectives That Compare

Fill in each blank with the right form of the adjective in parentheses.

1. Otto is _____ than I am. (old)

2. His friend Al is the _____ player on the team. (young)

3. He is the _____ hitter in the league. (famous)

4. In our city, baseball is _____ than football. (popular)

5. The tickets for a baseball game are _____ too. (cheap)

Adjectives continued

Irregular Adjectives

Not all adjectives form comparisons in regular ways. The chart shows how to form common irregular adjectives.

Adjective	Comparative	Superlative
good, well	better	best
bad	worse	worst
many, much	more	most
little	less	least

Exercise: Irregular Adjectives

Fill in each blank with the right form of the adjective in parentheses.

1. I feel _____ today than I did yesterday. **(bad)**

2. This is the _____ cold I have ever had. **(bad)**

3. I have missed _____ days of school than my sisters. **(many)**

4. I am usually the _____ student. **(good)**

5. I usually miss the _____ amount of school. **(little)**

Double Comparisons

Never use *more* or *most* with an adjective that ends with *-er* or *-est*. This mistake in grammar is called a **double comparison.**

Wrong: My hometown is the <u>most</u> <u>bestest</u> place on earth.
Right: My hometown is the <u>best</u> place on earth.

Wrong: It is <u>more</u> <u>warmer</u> here than in Miami.
Right: It is <u>warmer</u> here than in Miami.

Exercise: Double Comparisons

Highlight and fix the four adjective mistakes.

(1) I like comedies more better than dramas. (2) To me, nothing is funnier than slapstick comedies. (3) I laugh the most hardest at physical comedians, like Jim Carrey. (4) He makes the most craziest faces! (5) I feel more happier after I watch one of his movies.

Adverbs

Adverbs describe verbs, adjectives, and other adverbs. Adverbs answer these questions: *How? When? Where? How much? How often?*

How: Jim spoke <u>quietly</u>.

When: He is <u>never</u> loud.

Where: He arrived <u>here</u> at five o'clock.

How much: He was <u>too</u> late.

How often: He <u>usually</u> arrives at four o'clock.

The *-ly* Adverb Ending

Many adverbs are formed by adding *-ly* to the end of an adjective.

Example: quiet + ly = quietly

Not all adverbs end in *-ly*, however, and not every word that ends in *-ly* is an adverb. For example, the word *friendly* ends in *-ly*, but it is an adjective, not an adverb.

> The word *real* is an adjective. The word *really* is an adverb. Use *really* when you are describing an adjective.
> **Wrong:** Sherelle is <u>real</u> happy.
> **Right:** Sherelle is <u>really</u> happy.

Exercise: The *-ly* Adverb Ending

Add *-ly* to each adjective in parentheses to form an adverb.

1. The receiver ran _____ down the field. **(graceful)**

2. The fans cheered _____. **(wild)**

3. They _____ stamped their feet. **(loud)**

4. He _____ neared the end zone. **(quick)**

5. The defense _____ ran after him. **(clumsy)**

6. He _____ placed the football in the end zone. **(happy)**

7. Then he _____ called out to the fans. **(joyous)**

8. They _____ chanted his name. **(repeated)**

Adverbs continued

Good and *Well*

Use the adjective *good* to describe people, places, and things.

Example: That is a good song.

Use *well* as an adverb to describe action verbs and adjectives. Use *well* as an adjective to describe someone's health.

Example: The band played well.

Example: Jen felt well after a good night's rest.

Exercise: *Good* and *Well*

Highlight and fix the two mistakes in the use of *good* and *well*.

(1) Mario did not feel good. **(2)** Therefore, he did not play good.

(3) He did make one good play, however.

Double Negatives

Do not form a **double negative** by using two negative words in one clause. The adverb *not* is negative, as are contractions that contain the word *not* (*can't, don't, haven't, isn't, wasn't, wouldn't,* and so on). To fix a double negative, change one of the negatives into a positive, or drop one of the negative words.

Wrong: I don't have no money.
Right: I don't have any money. OR I have no money.

Negatives	Positives
never	ever
nobody, no one	somebody, someone
none	some
nothing	something, anything
nowhere	somewhere
hardly, barely	_____

Exercise: Double Negatives

Highlight and fix the double negative in each sentence.

(1) Kelly didn't have hardly any money. **(2)** She couldn't afford to buy nothing. **(3)** I didn't have no money to lend her.

Prepositions

A **preposition** (pre puh ZI shuhn) shows the relationship between a noun or pronoun and another word in a sentence.

Example: The stars shone <u>above</u> us.
Example: We sat <u>on</u> a bench <u>beside</u> the lake.

Prepositions					
about	among	beneath	for	on	under
above	around	beside	from	onto	underneath
across	at	between	in	over	until
after	before	beyond	into	through	with
against	behind	by	near	to	within
along	below	during	of	toward	without

Prepositional Phrases

A **prepositional phrase** is a group of words that go together and that begin with a preposition and end with a noun or pronoun. The noun or pronoun at the phrase's end is the **object of the preposition.**

Prepositional Phrase: The moon rose <u>over the calm lake</u>.
preposition   object

Exercise: Prepositional Phrases

<u>Underline</u> the prepositional phrase in each sentence below.

(1) We decorated the school gym for our spring dance. (2) We covered cardboard stars with foil paper. (3) Two teachers hung the stars from the ceiling. (4) We taped colorful posters to the walls.

(5) The theme of the dance was "Spring Nights."

Conjunctions

Conjunctions (kuhn JUHNG shuhns) connect, or join, words or groups of words. There are three kinds of conjunctions:

1. coordinating

2. correlative

3. subordinating

Coordinating Conjunctions

Coordinating (koh AWR duh nay ting) **conjunctions** connect similar words or groups of words. They can link parts of sentences or whole sentences. The coordinating conjunctions are listed below.

Coordinating Conjunctions
and, but, for, nor, or, so, yet

Sentence Parts: Kim and her mom went on a trip.

Sentences: They went to Ohio, and they saw the Columbus Zoo.

Exercise: Coordinating Conjunctions

Highlight the coordinating conjunction in each sentence.

1. I like all holidays, but Thanksgiving is my favorite.

2. My grandparents come to my house, or we go to theirs.

3. We always have turkey, dressing, and cranberry sauce for dinner.

4. I do not mean to overeat, yet I always do.

5. I really like sweet potato pie, so my mom always bakes one.

6. I cannot bake, nor do I want to learn how.

7. I am spoiled, for my mom is such a good cook.

8. My grandmother and sister are also good cooks.

9. My dad likes barbecues, so he usually cooks for our Fourth of July celebration.

10. He makes barbecued ribs, and my mom makes potato salad.

Conjunctions continued

Subordinating Conjunctions

A **subordinating** (suh BOR duh nay ting) **conjunction** introduces and connects a subordinate clause to a main clause.

Subordinating Conjunctions			
after	because	since	until
although	before	so that	when
as	even though	than	where
as if	if	though	whereas
as though	in order that	unless	while

Example: While we were in Chicago, we visited museums.

                  subordinate clause   main clause

Exercise: Subordinating Conjunctions

Highlight the subordinating conjunction in each sentence and underline the subordinate clause.

(1) Though Janelle is my twin, we are very different. **(2)** While

I like sports, she likes music. **(3)** I cover my ears whenever she sings.

(4) I act as if she is the worst singer on earth. **(5)** I tease her just

because she is my sister.

Correlative Conjunctions

Correlative (kuh RE luh tiv) **conjunctions** work in pairs.

Correlative Conjunctions	
both . . . and	either . . . or
not only . . . but also	neither . . . nor

Example: Both Lia and Raj are in the chess club.
Example: Neither Lia nor Raj likes to lose.

Exercise: Correlative Conjunctions

Highlight the pair of correlative conjunctions in each sentence.

(1) Both my sister and I want to be artists. **(2)** My sister not only

draws but also paints. **(3)** Neither my mom nor my dad is artistic!

Sentences

A **complete sentence** is a group of words that has a subject and a predicate and that expresses a complete thought. The **subject** tells who or what the sentence is about. The predicate tells what the subject is or does.

Complete Sentence: <u>Josephina</u> <u>overslept this morning</u>.

                subject   predicate

There are four types of sentences.

1. A **declarative** (di KLER uh tiv) sentence makes a statement.

- <u>Josephina</u> <u>missed</u> her bus.

2. An **imperative** (im PER uh tiv) sentence gives an order.

- <u>Set</u> the alarm. (The "understood" subject is <u>you</u>.)

3. An **exclamatory** (iks KLA muh tawr ee) sentence shows emotion.

- What a nightmare <u>she</u> <u>had</u>!

4. An **interrogative** (in tuh RAH guh tiv) sentence asks a question.

- What time <u>did</u> <u>she</u> <u>go</u> to bed last night?

Clauses

A **clause** is a group of words that contains a verb and its subject. A **main clause** can stand alone as a sentence. A **subordinate clause** begins with a subordinating conjunction. A subordinate clause cannot stand alone. It must be joined to a main clause.

Main clause: <u>Lenny</u> <u>is</u> afraid to speak in public.
Subordinate clause: because <u>he</u> <u>is</u> very shy.
Sentence: Lenny is afraid to speak in public because he is very shy.

Exercise: Clauses

<u>Underline</u> the main clause in each sentence below.

(1) After we do our homework, my brother and I usually watch TV.

(2) We often argue because we do not like the same TV shows.

(3) While I like mysteries, he likes comedies. **(4)** Sometimes, I grab the remote control before he does. **(5)** When I control the TV, we watch detective shows.

Sentences continued

Run-on Sentences

A **run-on sentence** is a common kind of mistake in writing. A run-on happens when two or more sentences are written as one sentence. There are three kinds of run-on sentences:

1. Main clauses are separated only by a comma.

- Roy walked home, it was autumn.

2. Main clauses are not separated by any punctuation.

- The sky was blue the leaves were red and gold.

3. Main clauses are separated by a coordinating conjunction, but the comma before the conjunction is missing.

- He felt like running but he did not want to make any noise.

Here are two ways to fix a run-on sentence:

Fix 1: Separate the main clauses, or sentences, with a period.

- Roy walked home. It was autumn.

Fix 2: Add a comma and a coordinating conjunction (if the sentences are not already separated by a coordinating conjunction).

- The sky was blue, and the leaves were red and gold.

- He felt like running, but he did not want to make any noise.

Exercise: Run-on Sentences

Fix the four run-on sentences below. There is more than one right way to fix each sentence.

(1) Ice cream has a long history it has probably been around for thousands of years. (2) The first ice cream did not contain cream, it was made of fruit and ice. (3) A king of ancient China mixed ice with milk and the recipe for this tasty treat was brought to Europe. (4) European royalty served ice cream at dinner parties ice cream became fashionable. (5) Ice cream was once too expensive for ordinary people, but now just about everybody enjoys it.

Sentences continued

Fragments

A **sentence fragment** is an incomplete sentence that is capitalized and punctuated as if it were complete. Common reasons for fragments are as follows:

1. The sentence is missing a subject.

Fragment: <u>Went</u> to a storytelling festival.
Complete: <u>Al and Beatrice went</u> to a storytelling festival.

2. The sentence is missing a predicate.

Fragment: <u>Al and Beatrice</u> to a storytelling festival.
Complete: <u>Al and Beatrice went</u> to a storytelling festival.

3. A subordinate clause is not connected to a main clause.

Fragment: When they got to the festival.
Complete: When they got to the festival, <u>they saw some friends.</u>

Exercise: Fragments

Follow the directions in parentheses to fix each fragment.

1. (Add a subject.) Have been working hard.

2. (Add a predicate.) A big social studies project due.

3. (Add a main clause.) if it is not done on time

4. (Add a predicate.) Where the library?

5. (Add a main clause.) Since librarians are information experts.

_____

_____

Capitalization

Capitalize proper nouns and proper adjectives. A **proper noun** names a specific person, place, or thing. A **common noun** does not. A **proper adjective** is an adjective formed from a proper noun.

Common	Proper
man	Damion
street	Sloan Street
school	Wilson Middle School

Capitalization Rules

Capitalize the following.

1. The proper name or title of a person.
   - Sue, Dad, Ms. Smith, Detective Jones, President Adams

2. The proper name of a place.
   - Chicago, Utah, France, Main Street, the Sears Tower

3. A proper adjective.
   - American, Mexican, Chinese

4. The first word of a sentence.
   - The night was dark.

5. A letter's salutation and the first word of the closing.
   - Dear Sir: • Sincerely yours,

6. The first word, last word, and all main words in the title of a work.
   - *The Sound of Music*

Exercise: Capitalization

Highlight and fix the capitalization mistake or mistakes in each numbered line.

(1) Dear uncle Joey,

(2) We are in New York city! (3) Today, we went to Ellis island.

(4) We visited the Museum there. (5) Then we ate at a Chinese

Restaurant. (6) tomorrow we will see a play. (7) It is called

Guys And Dolls.

Punctuation

Punctuation helps readers understand how sentences should be read. **Punctuation marks** include commas, apostrophes, quotation marks, and end marks (periods, question marks, exclamation points).

A **comma** signals a pause or separates parts of a sentence.
- When the phone rang, he answered.
- Berkeley, California, is her home.

An **apostrophe** can show possession, show where letters are missing in a contraction, or show that a letter or number is plural.
- Sara's ears almost froze when she didn't wear her hat.
- Several members of the class got straight A's.

Quotation marks set off someone's exact words. They are also used to set off titles of articles, short stories, and episodes of TV shows.
- "What did you say?" Homer asked.
- My favorite show is "My Best Friends."

End Marks

An **end mark** goes at the end of a sentence.
A **period** ends a complete sentence that makes a statement.
- Roz went to school early today.

A **question mark** ends a direct question.
- Why did she go early?

An **exclamation point** ends a sentence that shows strong emotion.
- Do not spill that juice!

 Put commas and periods inside closing quotation marks.
Example: "I am glad," Marcia said, "to meet you at last."

Exercise: End Marks

Add the correct end mark to each sentence.

(1) Have you ever swum in the ocean **(2)** I went swimming when we visited Florida **(3)** The ocean water was clean and warm **(4)** How beautiful the waves looked **(5)** My mom said, "This is very peaceful and relaxing" **(6)** I wonder if we will be able to go back there next year

Punctuation continued

Commas

Use commas in these situations:

1. To separate three or more items in a series.

- They walked past shops, houses, and parks.

2. To set off names and titles used in direct address.

- Have you seen my CD, Tim?   • No, Terrell, I haven't.

3. To set off dates and addresses.

- On July 25, 1999, my sister was born in St. George, Utah.

4. After an introductory word, phrase, or clause.

- Finally, the day ended.   • At last, we relaxed.   • If you want, sleep.

5. To set off groups of words that explain or rename.

- Felicia, our class president, does a good job.

- Soccer, my favorite sport, involves a lot of running.

6. To separate main clauses joined by a coordinating conjunction.

- Ron did his homework, but Ken did not do his.

Do not use a comma to separate a compound predicate.
Wrong: Ron sings well, and plays the guitar even better.
Right: Ron sings well and plays the guitar even better.

Exercise: Commas

Add the missing comma or commas to each sentence.

(1) Terry do you know what Cinco de Mayo is? **(2)** Though it is a Mexican holiday many Americans also celebrate it. **(3)** A battle took place on May 5 1862 in Puebla Mexico. **(4)** On that date Mexican troops fought invading French troops. **(5)** Ignacio Seguín Zaragosa a great general led the Mexicans to victory. **(6)** Cinco de Mayo or May Fifth commemorates this victory. **(7)** Some families celebrate by feasting listening to music and dancing. **(8)** Even if you are not Mexican you can join the fiesta.

Punctuation continued

Apostrophes

Use an apostrophe to show where letters are missing in a contraction.
• aren't (are not), can't (cannot), haven't (have not).

Also use an apostrophe to show possession.
• Cal's dad drove him to school. Some kids' parents drive to school.

Do not confuse contractions with possessives that sound like them. A possessive pronoun never takes an apostrophe.
• The cat licked its fur, and now it's clean.

Exercise: Apostrophes

Fix the apostrophe mistake in each sentence.

(1) Steves favorite video game is Soap Box Derby. (2) Its a cross between racing cars and building race cars. (3) Hes playing the game right now. (4) May I borrow your's?

Quotation Marks

Use quotation marks before and after someone's exact words. Do not use them to set off an indirect quotation.

Direct quotation: "I'm ready," Shari said, "to work."
Indirect quotation: Shari said she was ready to work.

Set off titles of articles, short stories, and episodes of TV shows with quotation marks.

Title of Essay: Did you read the article "Sports Shorts"?
Title of Story: My favorite story is "Amigo Brothers."

Exercise: Quotation Marks

Add quotation marks where needed in the sentences below.

1. Did you do your homework? Mickey asked.

2. We are supposed to read the story Two Kinds.

3. I started to read it, Bob said, but I fell asleep.

Spelling

Though some words are spelled exactly the way they sound, many are not. Use these rules to help guide your spelling. When in doubt, turn to a dictionary for help.

1. Put *i* before *e* except after *c* or the sound "ay."

Examples: bel*ie*ve, fr*ie*nd, p*ie*ce, rel*ie*f, sh*ie*ld
Examples: c*ei*ling, re*cei*pt, re*cei*ve, n*ei*ghbor, w*ei*ght

2. When adding an ending that starts with a vowel (like *-ed*, *-er*, or *-ing*), double these final consonants: *b, d, g, l, m, n, p, r,* and *t.*

Examples: sob*bed*, nag*ged*, begin*ner*, win*ner*, tap*ping*, bat*ting*

3. When adding *-ed*, *-es*, *-ing*, or *-y* to a word that ends with a silent *e*, drop the *e*.

Examples: bake + *-ed* = bak*ed*, tape + *-ing* = tap*ing*, rose + *y* = ros*y*

4. When a word ends in a consonant plus *y*, change the *y* to *i* before adding an ending like *-ed*, *-es*, *-est*, or *-ly*.

Examples: supply + *-ed* = suppl*ied*, fly + *-es* = flies,
easy + *-est* = eas*iest*, happy + *ly* = happ*ily*

5. When a word ends in a vowel plus *y*, do not change the *y* to *i* when adding *-ed*, *-er*, or *-s*.

Examples: del*ay*ed, pl*ay*er, s*ays*, k*eys*, t*oys*, g*uys*

Exercise: Spelling

Highlight and fix the spelling mistake in each sentence.

(1) Coach, did you recieve the shipment of shoes for the soccer team? (2) Did you order the other supplys we need? (3) My nieghbor Lonny wants to play this year. (4) Last year, he played sloppyly. (5) This year he amazeed me with his speed. (6) Also, Sal's footwork is dazzleing. (7) All the plaiers are ready for the season. (8) Some of the guyes have been training for months. (9) This will be the crazyest season ever for our team. (10) I predict that we'll be winers by December.

Commonly Confused Words

The words on this list give many writers trouble. Use the list for help in figuring out the right word to use.

accept, except
Accept means "to agree to" or "to welcome." *Except* means "but."

- I hope everyone will <u>accept</u> the new student to our class.
- We go to school every day <u>except</u> Saturday and Sunday.

affect, effect
Affect means "to influence" or "to have an impact on." *Effect* means "result."

- I hope the cancelled flight will not <u>affect</u> your travel plans.
- A high fever was one <u>effect</u> of the disease.

a lot
The expression *a lot* means "a large number" or "a large amount." It must be written as two words.

- <u>A lot</u> of people came to the championship game.

all ready, already
The expression *all ready* means "completely prepared." It is written as two words. *Already* means "before now." It is one word.

- Dinner was <u>all ready</u> by the time the guests arrived.
- I got to the stadium so late the game was <u>already</u> over.

amount, number
The word *amount* describes a quantity that cannot be counted. Use *number* to describe things that can be counted.

- The cake contained a large <u>amount</u> of sugar.
- She was impressed by the <u>number</u> of tickets that were sold.

beside, besides
Beside refers to someone or something that is next to something else. *Besides* means "as well as" or "other than."

- She stood <u>beside</u> the lamppost, waiting for the bus.
- <u>Besides</u> math, I also like to study science and English.

Commonly Confused Words continued

can, may
The verb *can* means "is able to." *May* means "allowed to."

- She <u>can</u> repair the car because she has the right tools.
- He <u>may</u> watch the concert because he has a ticket.

fewer, less
Fewer compares numbers of people or things that can be counted.
Less compares amounts or quantities that cannot be counted.

- The class had <u>fewer</u> boys than girls.
- My new car uses <u>less</u> gas than my old one.

like, as
Like is a preposition and should be followed by an object. *As* is a subordinating conjunction and should be followed by a clause, which contains both a subject and a verb.

- She sings <u>like</u> a bird.
- She sings <u>as</u> a <u>bird</u> <u>would sing</u>.

loose, lose
Loose is an adjective (meaning "weakly connected" or "unattached"), or it is a verb (meaning "set free" or "untied"). *Lose* is always a verb (meaning the opposite of "to win" or "to find").

- The <u>loose</u> stones in the wall fell to the street.
- The team that does not practice is sure to <u>lose</u> the game.

rise, raise
Rise means "to go up." *Raise* is used with an object, and it means "to lift or force up."

- The sun will <u>rise</u> at seven o'clock tomorrow morning.
- Please <u>raise</u> your hand if you have a question.

sit, set
Sit means "to be seated." *Set* means "to put or place."

- I will <u>sit</u> at the table during dinner.
- I will <u>set</u> the dishes on the table.

Commonly Confused Words continued

than, then

Than is a subordinating conjunction used to compare one person or thing with another. *Then* is an adverb that means "after that" or "next."

- An elephant is larger <u>than</u> a mouse.
- First beat the eggs, and <u>then</u> add the milk.

their, there, they're

Their is a possessive pronoun, which is used to show that something belongs to someone. The adverb *there* is used to express where something is. *They're* is the contraction for *they are*.

- <u>They're</u> going to swim during <u>their</u> visit to Florida.
- The weather is sunny and warm <u>there</u>.

to, too, two

To expresses a direction or location. *Too* means "as well" or "in addition." *Two* is the number between one and three.

- I bought <u>two</u> tickets for the concert, so you can come, <u>too</u>.
- We should take a bus <u>to</u> the theater.

who, whom

Who is the subject of a verb. *Whom* is an object, either receiving the action of a verb or ending a prepositional phrase.

- <u>Who</u> wrote the letter?
- <u>Whom</u> did Bob call?
- For <u>whom</u> did you ask?

who's, whose

Who's is a contraction meaning "who is." *Whose* is a possessive pronoun, expressing ownership or relationship.

- <u>Who's</u> going to be our teacher next year?
- Do you know <u>whose</u> bicycle this is?

Editing Checklist

Use this checklist as you edit your writing. (You can also use this checklist to edit a partner's work.) Keep track as you complete each step.

1. I found misspelled words and used strategies to spell them correctly.

2. I checked to be sure that I used the correct homophone, such as *your/you're*, *to/too/two*, and *they're/their/there*.

3. I reread each sentence to make sure that I did not leave out words.

4. I fixed run-on sentences and sentence fragments.

5. I looked to be sure that each new idea started a new paragraph.

6. I correctly placed periods, question marks, exclamation marks, and commas where they belong.

7. I began each sentence with an uppercase letter.

8. I used uppercase letters for names of people and places and for proper nouns.

9. I made sure that subjects and verbs in sentences agree.

My editing goals:

_____

_____

_____

_____

_____

_____

Proofreaders' Marks

Use these marks as you review your own or a partner's writing.

⟍	Delete	∧	Insert here
◡	Close up; delete space	⋀	Insert comma
(stet)	Let it stand	⋁	Insert apostrophe
#	Insert space	⋁ ⋁	Insert quotation marks
¶	Begin new paragraph	⊙	Insert period
(sp)	Spell out	(set)?	Insert question mark
(lc)	Set in lowercase	◇	Insert colon
(caps)	Set in capital letters	=	Insert hyphen

Dear Jurors⋀

I think you should put you're trust in forensic science⊙
One reason for is that a witness to a crime may not
rember all the details. Proove from science is reliable. Its
hard to argue with a fingerprint or dna. Another reason
is that science keeps getting gooder. Compared to a
long time ago scientists can find out more information.
About crime scenes. If you were accused of a crime,
wouldn't you want science on your side.

Personal Word Bank

Use the Word Bank to keep track of the "Your Choice" words from the articles.

For each word you add, do the following:

- Write the word in the box.
- Rate how well you understand it.

  1 = I do not know this word.

  2 = I have seen or heard this word.

  3 = I could use this word in a sentence.

  4 = I could teach this word to someone else.

- Write the definition in your own words.
- Write an example of the word or a connection you have with it.
- Use the word! Write with it, speak with it, and pay attention if you find it in your reading. Then go back to your rating and see if you can improve it.

Word: _____	My Understanding 1 2 3 4

Definition: _____

Example or Connection: _____

_____

_____

Word: _____	My Understanding 1 2 3 4

Definition: _____

Example or Connection: _____

_____

_____

Word: _____	My Understanding 1 2 3 4

Definition: _____

Example or Connection: _____

_____

_____

Word: _____	My Understanding 1 2 3 4

Definition: _____

Example or Connection: _____

_____

_____

Word: _____	My Understanding 1 2 3 4

Definition: _____

Example or Connection: _____

_____

_____

Word: _____	My Understanding 1 2 3 4

Definition: _____

Example or Connection: _____

_____

_____

Personal Word Bank

Word: _____	My Understanding 1 2 3 4

Definition: _____

Example or Connection: _____
_____
_____

Word: _____	My Understanding 1 2 3 4

Definition: _____

Example or Connection: _____
_____
_____

Word: _____	My Understanding 1 2 3 4

Definition: _____

Example or Connection: _____
_____
_____

Word: _____	My Understanding 1 2 3 4

Definition: _____

Example or Connection: _____
_____
_____

Word: _____	My Understanding 1 2 3 4

Definition: _____

Example or Connection: _____
_____
_____

Word: _____	My Understanding 1 2 3 4

Definition: _____

Example or Connection: _____
_____
_____

Word: _____	My Understanding 1 2 3 4

Definition: _____

Example or Connection: _____
_____
_____

Word: _____	My Understanding 1 2 3 4

Definition: _____

Example or Connection: _____
_____
_____

Word: _____	My Understanding 1 2 3 4

Definition: _____

Example or Connection: _____
_____
_____

Word: _____	My Understanding 1 2 3 4

Definition: _____

Example or Connection: _____
_____
_____

Personal Word Bank

Word: _____ | My Understanding
Definition: _____ 1 2 3 4
Example or Connection: _____
_____
_____

Word: _____ | My Understanding
Definition: _____ 1 2 3 4
Example or Connection: _____
_____
_____

Word: _____ | My Understanding
Definition: _____ 1 2 3 4
Example or Connection: _____
_____
_____

Word: _____ | My Understanding
Definition: _____ 1 2 3 4
Example or Connection: _____
_____
_____

Word: _____ | My Understanding
Definition: _____ 1 2 3 4
Example or Connection: _____
_____
_____

Word: _____ | My Understanding
Definition: _____ 1 2 3 4
Example or Connection: _____
_____
_____

Word: _____ | My Understanding
Definition: _____ 1 2 3 4
Example or Connection: _____
_____
_____

Word: _____ | My Understanding
Definition: _____ 1 2 3 4
Example or Connection: _____
_____
_____

Word: _____ | My Understanding
Definition: _____ 1 2 3 4
Example or Connection: _____
_____
_____

Word: _____ | My Understanding
Definition: _____ 1 2 3 4
Example or Connection: _____
_____
_____

Personal Word Bank

	My Understanding
Word: _____	1 2 3 4

Definition: _____

Example or Connection: _____
_____
_____

	My Understanding
Word: _____	1 2 3 4

Definition: _____

Example or Connection: _____
_____
_____

	My Understanding
Word: _____	1 2 3 4

Definition: _____

Example or Connection: _____
_____
_____

	My Understanding
Word: _____	1 2 3 4

Definition: _____

Example or Connection: _____
_____
_____

	My Understanding
Word: _____	1 2 3 4

Definition: _____

Example or Connection: _____
_____
_____

	My Understanding
Word: _____	1 2 3 4

Definition: _____

Example or Connection: _____
_____
_____

	My Understanding
Word: _____	1 2 3 4

Definition: _____

Example or Connection: _____
_____
_____

	My Understanding
Word: _____	1 2 3 4

Definition: _____

Example or Connection: _____
_____
_____

	My Understanding
Word: _____	1 2 3 4

Definition: _____

Example or Connection: _____
_____
_____

	My Understanding
Word: _____	1 2 3 4

Definition: _____

Example or Connection: _____
_____
_____

Personal Word Bank

Word: _____ | My Understanding
                                   1 2 3 4

Definition: _____

Example or Connection: _____
_____
_____

Word: _____ | My Understanding
                                   1 2 3 4

Definition: _____

Example or Connection: _____
_____
_____

Word: _____ | My Understanding
                                   1 2 3 4

Definition: _____

Example or Connection: _____
_____
_____

Word: _____ | My Understanding
                                   1 2 3 4

Definition: _____

Example or Connection: _____
_____
_____

Word: _____ | My Understanding
                                   1 2 3 4

Definition: _____

Example or Connection: _____
_____
_____

Word: _____ | My Understanding
                                   1 2 3 4

Definition: _____

Example or Connection: _____
_____
_____

Word: _____ | My Understanding
                                   1 2 3 4

Definition: _____

Example or Connection: _____
_____
_____

Word: _____ | My Understanding
                                   1 2 3 4

Definition: _____

Example or Connection: _____
_____
_____

Word: _____ | My Understanding
                                   1 2 3 4

Definition: _____

Example or Connection: _____
_____
_____

Word: _____ | My Understanding
                                   1 2 3 4

Definition: _____

Example or Connection: _____
_____
_____

Personal Word Bank

Word: _____
My Understanding
1 2 3 4

Definition: _____

Example or Connection: _____
_____
_____

Word: _____
My Understanding
1 2 3 4

Definition: _____

Example or Connection: _____
_____
_____

Word: _____
My Understanding
1 2 3 4

Definition: _____

Example or Connection: _____
_____
_____

Word: _____
My Understanding
1 2 3 4

Definition: _____

Example or Connection: _____
_____
_____

Word: _____
My Understanding
1 2 3 4

Definition: _____

Example or Connection: _____
_____
_____

Word: _____
My Understanding
1 2 3 4

Definition: _____

Example or Connection: _____
_____
_____

Word: _____
My Understanding
1 2 3 4

Definition: _____

Example or Connection: _____
_____
_____

Word: _____
My Understanding
1 2 3 4

Definition: _____

Example or Connection: _____
_____
_____

Word: _____
My Understanding
1 2 3 4

Definition: _____

Example or Connection: _____
_____
_____

Word: _____
My Understanding
1 2 3 4

Definition: _____

Example or Connection: _____
_____
_____